Prais[

More Perfect Union?:

'Alan Wilson is the only bishop in the Church of England who speaks for the full inclusion of LGBTQI people in the Church. In this powerful statement, he sets out the scientific, theological and Biblical reasons which have led him to believe that this is the truly Christian option.'

Linda Woodhead MBE, Professor of Sociology of Religion, Lancaster University, and Organiser of the Westminster Faith Debates

'Alan Wilson says his aim in this book is to "help people with moral and Christian instincts about marriage to synchronise their heads and their hearts about gay people marrying". Except with the most congealed hard-liners, I think he will succeed. He covers the necessary theological ground – the biblical material and an analysis of the changing patterns of marriage through history – with freshness and energy. His analysis of the "narrow gauge" of Scripture (the usual killer verses) alongside the "broad gauge" derivation of ethics from the whole sweep of Scripture is particularly enlightening; and his conclusion is compelling – that the deep relational and spiritual sense that Scripture assigns to marriage does not and never did depend on gender difference or procreation.

'The theology is thoroughly and persuasively done; but the contemporary comment is devastating. The joy of this book is a bishop telling the truth, not least about the way the gay issue has been handled in recent history, and the awful dishonesties in which we are now entrammelled as a result. There is an especially relevant chapter on Geopolitics and Mission. How does the Church create "good disagreement" within the worldwide family? Not by scapegoating vulnerable minorities, or capitulating to the blackmail of threats of schism. Why should gay people demand marriage and not be content with the Church's (belated and partial) acceptance of civil partnership? Because accepting civil partnership but not marriage is like letting black people on to the bus but still making them sit at the back.

'There is some anger here, but the point is always positive: Wilson is an apostle of Christ, not a secular liberal. At the heart of the scriptural and traditional doctrine of marriage is a profound truth for all time which must be shared with all, and the Church's present stance is a block to the Gospel. As Augustine saw, a Christian vocation to marriage is distinguished by characteristics of permanence, stability and fidelity, reflecting the covenanted grace of God to his people – and that applies to a same sex marriage as much as to any other. Teaching this, in Wilson's words, "is now integral to bringing the grace and truth of Christ to this generation".'

Dr Jeffrey John, Dean of St Albans

'Few people have the perspective on LGBT issues in the Church that Bishop Alan Wilson does. Even fewer have shown as much selfless concern. In this new book Alan draws on his experience both as a bishop but also as a Christian who has personally lived in both the "for" and "against" gay marriage camps. He also draws on a smorgasbord of theologians, philosophers and modern thinkers to deliver this passionate and insightful work. Whether you agree with his conclusions or not, this could never be a dull read and I promise it will spur you to think about your own perspectives on this important debate!'

The Revd Sally Hitchiner, Senior Chaplain at Brunel University and Founder of Diverse Church

'Whatever your opinion on the issue of same sex marriage – this book is for you. For all who have an open and enquiring mind, Alan Wilson poses thought-provoking questions, challenges long assumed "truths" and sheds huge amounts of light on some entrenched misconceptions about marriage, the Bible and our cultural history. An extraordinarily valuable contribution to the quest for an open and honest conversation around an issue that the Church can no longer sweep under the ecclesiastical carpet.'

The Revd Steve Chalke MBE, Founder, Oasis Global and Stop The Traffik, United Nations Special Advisor on Community Action Against Human Trafficking

'How refreshing to listen to a bishop talking common sense about sexuality. This book presents the Church of England with stark reality, and sees it as good news. Readers well beyond Anglicanism will greatly benefit from its clear-sighted analysis.'

Diarmaid Macculloch, Professor of the History of the Church, University of Oxford

'In this remarkably honest account of his own personal journey, Alan Wilson offers a clear analysis of the matters that the Church needs to address on same-sex marriage and related issues. Informed by insights from many disciplines, he sets the discussion in its historical and cultural context and in the process offers a masterclass on biblical hermeneutics and practical theology. Some will undoubtedly find his conclusions unacceptable, but few will deny that he has identified the key questions that the Church should be thinking about and in doing so has set the agenda for informed discussion of the way forward.'

John Drane, Professor of New Testament and Practical Theology, Fuller Seminary, and Fellow of St John's College, University of Durham

'Alan Wilson has written an intelligent and measured account of the current state of thinking in the Anglican Church about same-sex marriage. This is an issue with which the Church will have to grapple towards acceptance. I concluded my speech in the House of Lords on the Bill in June 2013 with the comment about the Church's determination to stand aside from this liberalisation with the words:

"St Paul wrote to the Galatians that in Jesus Christ there is neither male or female, gentile or Jew, slave or free. I do not think that that was a coded message that everybody was okay except gays. It was an inclusive statement. As a member of the Anglican world, I hope that one day, before I die, I will see the Anglican Church unlock that quadruple lock from the inside..."

'I think Alan Wilson's book may represent the sound of the key being fitted to the lock.'

Ian, Lord Blair of Boughton

'Alan Wilson has written a highly readable and at times racy book on same-sex marriage in the Church of England. It is an invaluable resource for everyone in the Church, whatever their opinion about equal marriage. It will be of particular value to lesbian and gay Christians and our bisexual, transgender, intersex and straight friends, because it deals with biblical, theological, historical, pastoral and social issues that affect us all, covering all the bases.

'Bishop Alan has written from personal experience with honesty and truth, bringing clarity to the Church's inadequate grasp of the equality and prejudice which is poisoning its mission and ministry in a society which has largely overcome negative attitudes to sexual and gender diversity.

'*More Perfect Union?* articulates and challenges the thinking and theology of many of his brother bishops in the Church of England. If only they could find a similar commitment to speak the truth in public.

'The concluding chapter accurately surveys the current situation. Here and in previous chapters, misconceptions about marriage, Scripture and especially the legal situation as it applies to equal marriage are corrected and explained. This will provide proper information for lesbian and gay laity and clergy in the Church, and a salutary reminder as to why the present situation is intolerable.

'Above all, the book does justice to the experience and expectations of LGBTI Christians. It concludes with a helpful acknowledgment of the incompatibility of positions in the Church in which simplistic binary views are adopted. Bishop Alan notes that the doctrine of the Church of England is clear in theory but ambivalent in practice. Given that doing nothing is not an option, he asks: "How is the Church going to respond to the demand for same-sex marriages?"

'This is a deeply realistic and ultimately an optimistic book. As Bishop Alan says in his concluding paragraph, "The gold standard for human relationships is not control or hierarchy, but self-giving love".'

The Revd Colin Coward MBE, Director of Changing Attitude England

'This firefly of a bishop, buzzing with the light of faith and the courageous energy of a pastor, sets out his contribution to the debate the Church now faces: should we have a theology of marriage that more fully reflects the love of God for everyone? Like him, I believe we should cherish the sacrament of marriage by opening it to all loving couples, whether gay or straight, just as we have more recently opened the sacrament of ordination to women as well as men. God's love always ends up surprising us into new demands. Whether you finally agree with Bishop Alan or not, the Christian integrity of his argument is clear and invites a robust engagement and a greater honesty than the Church has yet managed on issues of human relationships and sexuality.'

Canon Mark Oakley, Chancellor, St Paul's Cathedral

More Perfect Union?

Understanding Same-Sex Marriage

Alan Wilson

DARTON · LONGMAN + TODD

First published in 2014 by
Darton, Longman and Todd Ltd
1 Spencer Court
140 – 142 Wandsworth High Street
London SW18 4JJ

ISBN: 978-0-232-53125-1

A catalogue record for this book is available from the British Library.

Phototypeset by Kerrypress Ltd, Luton, Beds
Printed and bound by Bell & Bain, Glasgow.

Contents

Preface

This book describes a stage in an ongoing journey towards equality. All over the world marriage is being opened to gay people. If Jesus' disciples' ideals about loving God and others are to take flesh, how can we be doers as well as hearers of the word (James 1:12)? As legislation for equal marriage in England drew near I had remarkable conversations that have resourced and informed what follows. I am really grateful to friends (some on Facebook), colleagues and campaigners for being honest, open and generous in sharing their experience, all of them in a personal rather than institutional capacity.

Naming names is invidious. Special thanks, however, to Peter Elliott, Andrew Foreshew-Cain, Linda Woodhead, Andrew Brown, Jeremy Pemberton, Laurence Cunnington, Mark Oakley, Simon Sarmiento, Paul Parker, Benny Hazelhurst, Steve Chalke, Jonathan Cooper, David Cameron, John Bercow, Joe Musgrave, Ann Memmott, Vicky Beeching, Kevin Holdsworth, Sally Hitchiner, Colin Coward, Erika Baker, Lucy Winkett, Nick Holtam, John Pritchard, David Percival, Richard Harries, Michael Ingham, Rupert Bursell, Barry Morgan, Diarmaid MacCulloch, Andrew Lightbown, Jane Shaw, Paul Fromberg, Grant Martin, Alex Dyer, Maggi Dawn, Martin Williams, Charlotte Methuen, Nigel Orchard, Karen Gorham, Mark Bennett, Olivia Graham, Jeffrey John, Norman Russell, Peter Southwell, Elizabeth Macfarlane, Michael Beasley, Liz Carmichael, Claire Jones, Joseph Pilling, Ian Blair, Alison Webster, David Porter, Ann Lee, Andrew Allen, Andrew Gear, Melissa Skelton, Rosemary Pearce, Andrew Proud, Colin Fletcher, David Walker, Rachel Mann, Richard Leggett, Will Stileman, Peter Ingrams, Julian Sullivan, Neil Turton, Ian Wills, Richard Holroyd,

Anne Davey, Sara Miles, Ruth Meyers, Christopher Lewis, John Rees, Andrew Johnson, Cathi Williams, Cole Moreton, Richard Coles, Phillip Giddings, Malcolm Johnson, Michael Marshall, Peter Ould, Richard Haggis, Louie Clay, Adrian and Megan Daffern, Ali Kaan, Giles Fraser, Sarah Meyrick, Luke Hopkins.

Particular thanks are due to my friend and close colleague Rosie Harper, who took an active part in almost all these conversations, and whose courage and clear thinking has shaped and immensely enriched what follows.

Home is the school of love. Some students asked me recently 'What is your greatest achievement?' I answered, instinctively, 'Marrying Lucy!' We have been fortunate to share over thirty years of close and joyful marriage. I owe great thanks also to our five wonderful children, Catherine, Stephanie, Stewart, Nick and Anna. We are rather a talkative family, and they've all contributed more than they probably realise.

Writing would not have been possible without the professional support of Catherine Green, my multitalented and long-suffering PA. I am also really grateful to David Moloney and Helen Porter of DLT for their vital roles in editing and producing this book.

This book is being finished where it began at Los Olivos, the Christian Retreat and Spirituality Centre in the Alpujarra mountains of Spain run by Dani Muñoz-Treviño and his husband Guy Wynter. It has been a place of enriched conversation, refreshment, exploration and beauty, all in the light of St John of the Cross, whose poems articulate love's subtle, surprising and glorious dimensions with heart-piercing clarity.

Los Olivos
Santiago Apóstol
25 July 2014

Outwitted?

One sunny morning in October 2003 I walked across Lambeth Bridge to Westminster Abbey and became an Anglican bishop. After 24 years' service as a parish priest in the Oxford Diocese, I was to become one of its bishops, serving the Archdeaconry of Buckingham. The week before someone had written me a card about bishops and unity quoting the Oregon poet Edwin Markham's famous epigram *Outwitted*:

> He drew a circle that shut me out –
> Heretic, a rebel, a thing to flout.
> But Love and I had the wit to win:
> We drew a circle that took him in!

What a vision for the job! The abbey was filled with a diverse array of people, including over five hundred churchwardens from Buckinghamshire. The liturgy expressed continuity with over a thousand years of faith in that place. The music was glorious. The shutters clicked, and the canapés afterwards were as inviting as they were plentiful. All around were warm friends and wonderful colleagues from my past, present and future.

One man's absence, however, and the injustice that caused it, was to haunt Anglican feasting in the following decade like Banquo's ghost in *Macbeth*.

Four months previously my wife Lucy and I had visited Lambeth Palace to begin the process of planning the consecration service. It was to be shared with a canon of Southwark Cathedral whose work as a Bible teacher I had greatly admired without having met him.

Dr Jeffrey John was nominated and had accepted to be the Bishop of Reading in my Oxford Diocese. Jeffrey struck

Lucy and me as a very pleasant and engaging man. I left our first meeting energised by the prospect of working alongside such a clear-thinking, gently humorous, wise and experienced colleague.

Within a few days, however a traditionalist backlash was in full swing, including from some of those who had been involved in Dr John's appointment. A vociferous campaign of personal abuse and vilification of his sexual orientation filled the papers. In what appeared to be a direct response to this, the Archbishop forced my ideal prospective colleague to withdraw his acceptance. All bets were off.[1]

Surely not, I thought. Our church does not behave like that. Dr John's life was entirely compliant with the official policy of celibacy for gays. The Church had repeatedly said we did not hold people's orientations against them. Only on this occasion, suddenly, we did. The Archbishop's official biography reveals someone whose primacy was affected throughout by the ramifications of what he had done, still anxious that he was legally vulnerable over discrimination years later.

What really got the campaigners' goats was that in 2000 the Canon had published a short book, *'Permanent, Faithful, Stable':* *Christian Same-Sex Partnerships,* arguing that the Church should recognise gay relationships for what they were. Its theological logic largely came from an essay by the Archbishop himself, *The Body's Grace,* published by the Lesbian and Gay Christian Movement in 1989, well before Dr Williams' elevation to Canterbury. Worse, they opined, as a gay man Dr John must have indulged in all kinds of unsavoury stuff in his time. They were not convinced, as they quaintly put it, that he had sufficiently repented of it, whatever it was.

I rather doubted that any expression of repentance would have satisfied some of those who were out to get him. Looking to my own life, were there any things I might have done thirty years before and insufficiently repented? As St Paul might have said, I was not aware of any, but that didn't mean they didn't exist.

How about 'the gay issue', as it was called? I was asked to sign the official policy, but with a caveat that most bishops understood its shortcomings better than they were able to admit publicly and it would develop in time. Bishops would have a special role, it was said, in helping the Church find its way forward. We were to try and head the troops off the battlefield and onto the mission field.

But how? First, I was told, we needed to clarify the terms of the debate. Too much rhetoric on all sides was vague, and boiled down in the end to 'yuk factors', or lack of them. Until very recently yuk factors were all around in English society. Now the Church's approach needed to be clearer, more honest and more clinical. I dusted off the single relevant essay I had written in 1978 as part of my theological college ethics course. I realised straight away how outdated my understanding of life science really was, and determined to mug up the facts of life afresh. What were their moral implications?

Secondly, a lot of fuss was being kicked up about a very few verses of the Bible. Conventional assumptions about the various terms' meanings were being read into the text, then out of it again. It was necessary to take Scripture more seriously than that. The Church needed courage to read the Bible as it was, but with fresh eyes. What possible interpretations might lead to progress and peace?

Thirdly, in the 1990s English people suddenly became far more open about personal matters. Some took the publicly expressed grief over Princess Diana's death in 1997 as a great sign that public emotional repression was lifting. The Church's approach to sex had been almost entirely implicit, with coded signals and allowances all round. If everyone began being open, light would shine in various closets. We could not expect things to carry on as they were. I needed to get to know gay people personally, especially Christians, listen to their experiences of love and life, and try to understand better what their lives were really about.

This book charts what I think I discovered from those explorations of life, Scripture and discipleship. It is not, in any sense, an academic tome. I asked myself, 'What does God want for gay people?' As I did this, it began to dawn on me it was no more than he wanted for all people – flourishing faith, hope and love, lived out individually and in community. There was no gay X factor. 'As a bishop,' I thought, 'why wait till you retire before you say what you really think? Why not try it now?'

For as long as possible I tried to be fair to all by perching on the fence. This became increasingly uncomfortable and, eventually, impossible. Those who run with the hare and hunt with the hounds, like all liars, need long memories and good luck. And, anyway, what's the point of lying? St Paul described a better way to live:

> Putting away falsehood, let all of us speak the truth to our neighbours, for we are members of one another. Be angry but do not sin; do not let the sun go down on your anger, and do not make room for the devil.
>
> (Ephesians 4:25–27)

Social ambivalence and duplicity ceased to be options once I realised there was no fence. I had to make up my mind about gay people, Scripture and its implications for life. In Christ, said St Paul, all God's promises are 'Yes!' and 'Amen!' (2 Corinthians 1:20). Making them 'Yes, but …' empties them of power and meaning. How would it be if I actually did the listening and discernment we were all supposed to have been doing for years, but without, apparently, having heard anything much?

Same-sex marriage crystallised the gay issue for me. It heralded the end for the gentlemen's club, with its 'don't ask, don't tell' silos. Marriage is a measurable reality, a public fact. People are married or they are not. This stark reality exposed as a sham the various hiding places the Church had devised down the years to evade the issue. The game was up.

In 2008 I first encountered friends abroad who were gay and married. I really wanted to share their joy. I did my best, but my head lagged behind my heart. This book explains how it caught up. I began to apply Scripture, tradition and reason to the issue. Allowing gay people to marry became not a matter of being nice to people but an issue of justice and equality. Rejoicing with gay people who marry, supporting them wholeheartedly, no longer seemed to me a concession to secular modernity, but sharing the good news of the kingdom.

I became increasingly open about my convictions on my blog and elsewhere. Some enriched Facebook conversations brought together people from all sides of the questions at issue. Soon I had heard from almost a thousand interested parties. I began to meet gay people, some of them living lives of extraordinary courage, integrity and resilience, often against a drab background of incomprehension and prejudice.

A minority of the straight people I encountered over this issue were diehard homophobes. I dislike the term intensely, but I can't think of another for people who tell you, in the name of God, that gay people are lice and vermin who should be aborted before birth. Disturbingly, bizarre homophobic rage always seemed to have a religious rationale. The very worst statements were often surrounded by bleating about how much God loves gay people really. If that's what he's trying to do, I thought, he has a funny way of showing it.

To my complete amazement, about 80 per cent of the messages I received after putting my head above the parapet were supportive. The vast majority of people seemed to be travelling along a road like mine, including a sizeable number of Evangelical Christians.

About nine out of ten of the people who disagreed strongly with me were bitter and angry, some bizarrely so. I was sent to hell several times. About one in ten of them were thoughtful and dialogued intelligently about a subject that troubled them rather than annoyed them. From this I learnt there was no necessary connection between Evangelical Christianity and prejudice, but much fear, perhaps, about naming the real latent issues.

A small minority of people I encountered were deeply prejudiced. As I got to know about them, I often discovered they had gay family members or unresolved issues around sexuality in their own lives. The vast majority of people who contacted me, however, were Christians basically trying to work out how to love their neighbour as themselves, struggling to understand changes in society around them, muddled but not malevolent.

Sex was never an easy subject to discuss with strangers. Most people's instincts were sincerely inclusive and understanding, but on their journeys towards equality, like mine, many people's heads lagged behind their hearts.

Sometimes Anglicans declared that every point of view in church about homosexuality has to be equally acceptable. The principle was like the one that whenever climate change was discussed on the BBC, a climate change denier had to be wheeled out and given 50 per cent of the airtime.

Having seen something of the ugly underside of ecclesiastical homophobia, I cannot agree. If the Church privileges prejudice, we will be stuck with it. One primary mission of a bishop in any church is to apply the Sermon on the Mount to all of life. I was amazed when an anonymous Mr Angry from Suffolk told me: 'It beggars belief that a bishop of the Church of England should suggest that the Sermon on the Mount could apply in any way to homosexuals.'

Jesus warned his followers, using the colourful language of the first century, that those who wilfully destroy their sisters or brothers for fools must answer for it in the fires of hell (Matthew 5:22). Bitter hatred, rage and wilful ignorance can never build a kingdom of justice, truth and love. The Church of England plays fast and loose with that principle at its peril.

Archbishop Robert Runcie used to say the Church is a swimming pool where most of the noise comes from the shallow end. My most lurid hate mail demonstrated the observation perfectly. It was a joy also to discover fellow disciples, including some Evangelicals and conservatives, who were not content to stay at the shallow end. I learnt how important it was not to make any assumptions about what people would say, and to frame the whole question around the needs of the whole community, not just its most strident and unreconstructed members.

My exploration has inevitably been an Anglican journey, but as I undertook it I met many other Christians with their own tensions, joys and challenges about sexuality. As Bishop of Buckingham, an area with strong Dissenting and Quaker traditions, it was a great joy to enlarge my understanding with members of the Society of Friends, along with many other individuals and groups. I am very sorry to say I encountered very little, if any, rooted homophobia outside Christian circles. This disturbing cloud does, however, have a silver lining. It may be that church leaders have special opportunities to challenge the religious roots of homophobia from within, rather than just attack it as a surface behaviour.

That is the real task. I managed to backfill some of the things that were missing when my head and heart were out of step about gay friends. Various Christians of my generation have told me about being invited to a same-sex wedding and wanting to join in wholeheartedly. All that held them back was a vague uneasiness, something to do with upbringing, conventional stereotypes and the hangover of thousands of years of fear and discrimination about gay people. I hope what I discovered, sometimes surprisingly, may help Christians to use resources from Scripture, tradition and reason to sync heart and head about their gay neighbours.

Wisdom is known by its fruits. I am sorry that the Church of England has not yet achieved corporate acceptance of married gay people. This is no niche issue but an integral part of the Church's core mission 'to bring the grace and truth of Christ to this generation and make him known to those within [our] care'.[2]

Gay and straight in Church and State

Can gay people marry?

It's a simple question, but English Christians are finding it almost impossible to ask, let alone answer. An overwhelming majority of English people have decided gay people's relationships should sometimes be legally recognised as marriages. Meanwhile, the Church of England remains the last bastion of 'eyes wide shut'. It is considered bad manners even to raise the subject in church. Yet it refuses to go away. Christians wonder where holiness might be found in a same-sex relationship. Can gay people, indeed, marry?

The Church of England faces special difficulties arising from its recent history. Fifty years ago everyone knew homosexuality was wrong. Now, most of the Church's active members no longer believe the official line. It is a gap that becomes more apparent every day.

Back in the 1950s and 60s, as homosexuality was being decriminalised in England, Church and State sang from the same hymn sheet. The Church was basking in what now seems like its twentieth-century heyday. Everyone agreed homosexuals could get married, of course, but only to someone of the opposite sex to whom they would not be attracted sexually. Homosexuality was viewed as an almost entirely male phenomenon. Lesbians were invisible.

Anxious parents, spiritual directors and teachers sometimes prescribed heterosexual marriage as a straightening-out strategy.

Homosexuality was believed to be a sin, a bad habit or, by more enlightened members of society, a tragic disability. Worried mothers and fathers really believed the right partner might straighten their gay sons out so that everyone could live happily ever after.

No one can wish anything but the best to those who tried this bold strategy in good faith if it worked for them in some way. In fact, few of these marriages did work out. Only a tiny minority of them apparently succeeded in their purpose. Even these usually inflicted serious damage on spouses and children along the way. Many lives were spoilt, even entirely ruined, by fumbling and fruitless pretending they were people they simply were not able to be. Failure as a husband rubbed salt into the wounds of failure to be a normal human being. The lucky ones got out when they realised the game was up. The 'marry a nice girl' strategy almost always failed.

Gay people often concluded, understandably, that there was something wrong with them. They sometimes escaped into a twilight world full of self-loathing, desperate concealment, furtive cottaging, promiscuity, depression, fear of blackmail, and the occasional suicide. The 1950s were no golden age for gay people, only for those who called them perverts. Some judged the horrors of this ghetto to be no less than its inhabitants deserved.

The Church of England handled homosexuality pastorally in two different ways.

The established Church played a big role in the apparatus of social disapproval. It had a strong mission to discourage homosexuality officially. Often seen as a kind of National Trust for British morals, bishops regarded their views on sex and marriage as the gold standard. Most people, churchgoers or not, agreed, even if imposing this morality sometimes seemed impractical or cruel.

Older teenagers saw marriage as the threshold of adult life. Wedlock was a licence for sexual activity, although many experimented illicitly before tying the knot. This moral obligation was borne out by Britain's Royal soap opera. Framed by the abdication crisis of 1937, in 1955 Princess Margaret, the Queen's younger sister, planned to marry Group Captain Peter Townsend, and was refused. The British establishment was not ready for the President of the Church of England Youth Council to marry a divorcee.

Homosexuality was seen as a form of social deviance. At the end of 1954 there were still over a thousand men in prison for gay-related sex offences. The Wolfenden Committee, which included the Anglo-Catholic Professor of Moral and Pastoral Theology at Oxford and a senior Church of Scotland minister, recommended decriminalisation in 1957, but it was ten years before Parliament summoned up the courage to enact it. Clergy generally saw homosexuality as either a tragic disability or a special kind of wickedness that called for a charitable but firm handling.

Unofficially the Church was sometimes kinder and more tolerant than society at large. The more gay clergy played the game by its largely unwritten rules the better they did. Eric Symes Abbott, for example, Warden of Keble College, ended up as chaplain to two sovereigns and Dean of Westminster.

Playing by the rules could be personally costly, however, when depression followed fearful dissimulation. Father Harry Williams became Dean of Trinity College Cambridge in 1958, but retreated to a monastery in 1967 after a series of spectacular mental breakdowns.

Almost all Evangelicals were either ignorant or hostile about gay people. Anglo-Catholics were more kind and tolerant in their own way, with a rich camp subculture in places, but founded on dogmatic inflexibility. There was no need to be unpleasant about it, but gayness was most definitely a disorder, the kind one should discuss with one's spiritual director.

These attitudes held up well within a broad social consensus that homosexuality was wrong and, until 1967, criminal.

Jaws dropped when Bryan Forbes' 1962 film *The L-Shaped Room* portrayed, for those with eyes to see, a gay black man and an ageing lesbian actress for the first time on British screens. Homosexuality was viewed as an almost entirely male phenomenon, reluctantly recognised as a besetting sin in schools, the entertainment industry and the armed services.

On stage, homosexuality was a matter of sniggering, salaciousness and pantomime dame *double entente*. Many popular entertainers' acts included ludicrous gay innuendoes and stereotypes, but in some ways these exacerbated the essential loneliness and misery of gay life. The popular actor and comedian Kenneth Williams discovered how important it was to keep mum about his private life, and his ended in despair and suicide.

The decriminalisation of homosexuality in 1967 set Britain on a 45-year cultural and legal path that one eminent family lawyer has described as 'from odious crime to gay marriage'.[1]

The Church, having often but not always played a progressive role before decriminalisation, spent the next ten years examining the subject. In 1979 a committee chaired by the Bishop of Gloucester reported, recommending modest reform. This provoked a hard backlash from some Evangelicals that was to drive church attitudes for the next 30 years.

On 11 November 1987, the General Synod passed what became known as the Higton Motion, after its original proposer, the Revd Tony Higton, an Essex clergyman. In its modified form, it said

> This Synod affirms that the biblical and traditional teaching on chastity and fidelity in personal relationships in a response to, and expression of, God's love for each one of us, and in particular affirms:
>
> 1. That sexual intercourse is an act of total commitment which belongs properly within a permanent married relationship;

2. That fornication and adultery are sins against this ideal, and are to be met by a call to repentance and the exercise of compassion;

3. That homosexual genital acts also fall short of this ideal, and are likewise to be met by a call to repentance and the exercise of compassion;

4. That all Christians are called to be exemplary in all spheres of morality, including sexual morality; and that holiness of life is particularly required of Christian leaders.

This introduced a curious new phrase to the language, that somehow said it all tastelessly, while saying nothing in particular – 'homosexual genital acts'. The motion's language about 'falling short of this ideal' was powerful enough, however, for it still to be in official use 27 years later by the bishop refusing a licence to Canon Jeremy Pemberton, the first gay clergyman to marry in England.

Heartened by a strong show in the General Synod, the next reactionary target was the 1989 Osborne Report. A group of theologians representing a broad range of thinking had proposed a modest process by which the Church's stance against gay people could be assessed biblically, doctrinally and pastorally. The prospect of this actually happening, however, enraged new-model conservatives, and the House of Bishops, terrified of another cringe-making debate in the General Synod, backed down and suppressed the report. It was banned for the next 25 years.

In gay history the mid-1980s saw the dawning of a decade dominated by AIDS. It brought to an end the first spring of gay rights agitation represented by the Stonewall Riots. Millions died. Fear brought the end of innocence. The disease struck people who had not come out, or were not supposed to.

Bishops of the London Diocese realised they knew little of the reality of gay clergy lives, and had no way to estimate the risk of AIDS deaths among their clergy. They called in the Revd Malcolm Johnson of St Botolph's, Aldgate, co-ordinator of the country's largest gay clergy network, to advise. Sensible provision was agreed, including a vicarage that could be used as a hospice if it were needed. Only two bishops in the room sat still and said nothing – interestingly enough, both were believed to be gay.[2]

Many gay rights activists of the Stonewall Riots era had experimented with radical ways of life carved out in sharp contradistinction to the marriages of their parents' generation. Hospice staff in the 1980s often discovered profound commitment between gay couples, sometimes in the face of hatred and denial from their partners' families. This began to change public perceptions of gay relationships as inherently casual, and opened people's eyes to their permanence and faithfulness, and the injustice of social rejection.

The Church of England, as usual ten years behind the beat, featured in *Simon's Cross*, a BBC *Everyman* documentary, first broadcast in January 1995. This movingly portrayed the South Yorkshire village of Dinnington and its rector, the Revd Simon Bailey. He learned that he had AIDS shortly before taking up the post, but worked unimpeded for seven years without obvious symptoms.

He led his community through the trauma of its pit closure, until he could no longer conceal his condition. After 1992 he told his parishioners openly and, far from condemnation, found a largely accepting response from them. The programme was a powerful affirmation of love and compassion within an ordinary community. It was a reminder of the human cost of AIDS, which some conservative Christians were glad to call a 'gay plague'. It demonstrated that the local church could rise above the national church's official policy of evasion, studied ambiguity and duplicity.

Among Anglicans the 1990s saw some official acknowledgment that change was in the air, but no real increase of understanding about homosexuality. It was often seen as some vague form of liberalisation, bracketed with feminism. Working parties worked, but their efforts were of no interest to the self-righteous conservative rump who wielded the whip hand in the 1990s. In 1998 an influential Evangelical, the Revd Michael Vasey (tutor at Cranmer Hall, Durham), died of AIDS-related complications, having published *Strangers and Friends*, a study that questioned the scanty biblical evidence against homosexuality. In general, though, the kind of real debate that had happened in the 1980s narrowed and progressively closed down during the decade.

Also in 1998, the Lambeth Conference attempted to broaden discussion across the Anglican Communion, but the process to do this was hijacked politically and neutralised. A tiny clique of reactionary activists played on largely ignorant fears and fantasies of third-world bishops like violins. The result, known as 'Lambeth 1.10', rejected homosexual practice as 'incompatible with Scripture', although it was coy about precisely the homosexual practice involved.

The Conference's most authentic but cringe-worthy media moment came when a Nigerian bishop, Emmanuel Chukwuma of Enugu, attempted (unsuccessfully) to exorcise the demon of homosexuality from the Revd Richard Kirker of the Lesbian and Gay Christian Movement. Kirker responded, with true Anglican self-restraint, 'God bless you, sir, and deliver you from your prejudice against homosexuality.'[3]

A church report, *Issues in Human Sexuality* (1991), had been intended to hold things at the status quo while discussions developed within it. Following the 1998 Lambeth Conference the document became a kind of Eleventh Commandment. That was that, and the Church of England hunkered down into a policy that was officially reactionary, but combined with unofficial collusion on a 'don't ask, don't tell' basis. The duplicity involved stank of hypocrisy, but not so much within the ecclesiastical bubble, whose skin would hold, it was believed, so long as no one breathed too hard.

Meanwhile, outside the bubble, new generations were taking a progressively more accepting, even affirmative, view of homosexuals. Almost every area of English life shifted in attitude around the turn of the twenty-first century. Section 28 of the Local Government Act 1988, controversial when it was passed, had nevertheless reflected a broad social consensus when it laid down that Local Authority schools, 'shall not intentionally promote homosexuality or publish material with the intention of promoting homosexuality', or, 'promote the teaching in any maintained school of the acceptability of homosexuality as a pretended family relationship'.

By 1998 the broad consensus of ten years before was creaking. Before much longer it seemed ludicrous to think such an offence, never alleged in court, was possible, let alone undesirable. The act was repealed in Scotland in 2000, and the rest of the United Kingdom in 2003. By 2008, with the passing of another generation, the majority consensus of 20 years before had simply evaporated.

The Church of England, officially, was now travelling in the opposite direction to the rest of society. As England signed up to cleaner more consistent human rights laws, the bishops instructed their lawyers to negotiate special opt-outs. Its General Synod was lost in its own factional internal politics, paralysed by a small reactionary clique exercising influence far beyond its numbers to hold various lines that were drawn in the sand. Surveying the scene, the Synod whined about its lost influence, complaining that the new government had no moral compass.[4]

As top brass painted themselves officially into a small corner, many of the troops were leaving the room in increasing numbers on the quiet. Between the censuses of 2001 and 2011, affiliation to the Church of England fell like a stone, especially among under fifties.

As the Church tried to freeze its view of gay people in the late 1970s, thaw set in elsewhere in society. Homophobia and hate crime still occurred on the streets, but public acceptance dawned in the law, politics, media, armed services, business and commerce, professional sport, education, art and design, technology, entertainment, healthcare and policing. All transitioned towards inclusion.

A new grouping began to emerge among the population, who now saw the Church of England as socially malign rather than irrelevant. This was not a matter of language or liturgy. Only 2 per cent cited that as the problem, and royal weddings remained as popular as ever, complete with 'thees and thous'. Sixteen per cent of this group found the Church toxic because of its obsession with hierarchy. A far larger group, however, 49 per cent of its members under 30, blamed its institutionalised sexism and homophobia. This evidence mirrored results of similar work undertaken in the USA by the Barna Institute, an Evangelical organisation charged with researching a supposedly lost generation of American Evangelical youth.

Rowan Williams, at the time he was appointed Archbishop of Canterbury in 2002, was well known to have advocated theological re-evaluation of homosexuality. It was hoped his learning and leadership would enable the Church to make the same kind of forward progress as other English public institutions at the time. Unfortunately, the institution ate the man for breakfast. This increased frustration on all sides.

Hope gave way to bitter disappointment all round, even among conservatives. Strong romantic attachment to the policy of 'back to the future' was not going to build a time machine capable of travelling back there. Society had moved on, and the underlying issues remained unresolved. Justin Welby, appointed Archbishop of Canterbury in 2013, was dealt a dreadful hand as regards homophobia, sexism and the Anglican Communion, all areas in which his predecessor's romantic management style had produced an angry shambles. It was time for a bit of holy pragmatism.

Back on Planet Earth, a government consultation on equal marriage was held in 2012. Of its 228,000 responses, 53 per cent agreed that couples should be able to have a civil marriage ceremony regardless of gender; 46 per cent disagreed, and 1 per cent were unsure or did not reply.

The Marriage (Same Sex Couples) Bill received the Royal assent on 17 July 2013, having secured large majorities in both Houses of Parliament. This shocked no one except a few right-wing journalists and the bishops of the Church of England. Similar enactments had obtained much the same-sized majorities in the previous 12 months in Brazil, France, Uruguay and New Zealand, along with 24 US jurisdictions from Hawaii to predominantly Catholic Maryland, from mostly Mormon Utah to the Pokagon Band of Potowatomi Indians.

The world seemed to be heading inexorably towards marriage equality. By 2014, 607 million people lived in a country with same-sex marriage. Every year the number was rising. There has been no serious proposal to reverse this reform in any country where it has been introduced. It does not seem the toothpaste will be going back into the tube.

In fact, in the noughties, the world was becoming more polarised. In 2014, homosexuality remained a criminal offence in 81 countries. Uganda and Nigeria passed draconian new legislation against gay people, with the enthusiastic backing of most local churches. Sometimes these were actively reinforced by Western missionaries.

Any serious consideration of same-sex marriage has to take account of recent increasing intercultural polarisation. This makes the question of same-sex marriage even harder to discuss or resolve.

People all over the world are often embarrassed to talk about sex and marriage. They are profoundly personal topics, often shrouded in custom, taboo and secrecy. They touch every level of what it means to be human – physical, social and spiritual. This is especially so in societies where people define themselves very much in relation to others. The African concept of Ubuntu says 'I am well if you are well'. In Western societies, where personal and family linkage is often more tenuous, personal relationships and coupling remain at the heart of social organisation.

In fast-changing societies, marriage provides significant stability for inherently volatile personal relationships. Marriage is the great means of generational handover. It brings together forces of personal continuity and change to secure the future. Fast developments in the public understanding of marriage, understandably, can inspire gut-level fear. Looking through a postbag arising from publicly standing up for gay people's right to marry, those with strong views about the subject on all sides have their own personal stories to tell.

This includes, of course, gay couples who have sometimes ploughed lonely furrows together for years without public understanding or sanction. Some of these couples have become desensitised to a point where the prospect of full recognition no longer matters. For others, societal endorsement of their relationships as marriage has powerfully reassured them of their equal place in society. A fair number of gay couples do not want to marry, of course, but for them the possibility of doing so has also been received as powerful social acknowledgement of them as the people they know themselves to be.

The burden of arguments about gay people being allowed to marry has always been carried disproportionately by them, because it is their relationships under the microscope. An ancient quip describes the levels of commitment required for bacon and eggs. The chicken gives all she has, but for the pig it's personal. He has to give what he is. This disproportionality needs to be borne in mind when the subject is discussed.

Because all sexuality is deeply personal it is not a dimension of life easily opened to strangers. Anyone discussing it is treading on other people's holy ground. People are not lab rats. The synodical and episcopal habit of talking *about* gay people instead of *with* them has helped make the basic question of same-sex marriage more destructive and insoluble. Any 'straights discussing gays' format is inherently offensive and useless.

Many who have publicly resisted same-sex marriage also have a dog in the fight arising from personal experience. This can arise from ambivalence or guilt about ways they have handled family members who have come out as gay, as well as their own sexualities. Particular attention sometimes falls on one vulnerable group with especially complex needs – gay Church of England bishops.

In 2003, Dr Jeffrey John was appointed Bishop of Reading, then vetoed by the Archbishop who had put him up for the job in the first place. His personal life was entirely compliant with Lambeth 1.10, but this was not enough to make him appointable. Being openly gay was the problem. The affair reinforced the policy of 'don't ask, don't tell.' By 2003, such dissimulation had become unnecessary for almost everyone else in UK working life. The Bishop of Reading incident made the Church of England look stupid and, even more damagingly, it clarified that being openly gay was still a disqualification regardless of a candidate's way of life or the official line on the subject. The result was to draw the bars firmly back across the inside of the episcopal closet door.

By 2014 there were said to be a dozen or so gay bishops. By definition, these men are outstanding priests who have managed to navigate the complexities of a structurally homophobic institution well enough to become its iconic representatives. They may well have a bigger investment than others in keeping the closet door tightly shut. Their existence sometimes causes resentment and anger to other gay people. What credibility can partnered gay bishops claim when they discipline partnered gay clergy for making their relationships legal?

The Church of England, like other national institutions before it, can only transition towards equality and inclusion with compassion and understanding all round. Particular unlearning is required of gay bishops. They have more on the line than some others. They also have greater status and security, but some of them may end up among the last people able to understand the need for change and bring it about. This can be expected to be the case especially for gay Evangelical bishops, with their historically less well developed networks and support systems.

Given recent history, with its raised stakes and increased polarisation, how can the Church consider the phenomenon of gay people marrying? Respect for the human dignity of everyone and the deeply personal nature of this question requires particular disciplines.

One practical necessity is not to slap on people terminology they do not accept for themselves. Sarcastic hostile terms like 'Fundamentalist', 'Revisionist' 'Evo' and even 'Liberal' (spat out with contempt) are only usable in so far as they are owned by the people to whom they are applied.

Secondly it is important to remember that times have changed radically since the facilitated conversations some dioceses held around the turn of the century. This is no longer a two-sided conversation between conservatives and liberals. It is four-sided, and the longest sides belong to people who are embarrassed to talk about it but realise change has happened, and the swelling company of those who have gay friends and family and simply can't see what the fuss is about. To most English people under 40 a discussion of gay bishops or same-sex marriage feels as relevant and inviting as one about women being allowed to drive in Saudi Arabia.

Better ways of disagreeing could, God willing, emerge from discussions about same-sex marriage. This can only happen if all participants listen to others who differ from them. The episcopal track record so far has been underwhelming – 30 years of listening, and many gay people can see no sign of their having corporately heard anything.

Issues in Human Sexuality (1991) called on senior Church leaders to listen to the experience of gay people. This has mainly been a one-way street. Gay people have sat demurely while their lordships discussed among themselves whether gays were who they thought they were or not. Bishops using homophobic rhetoric about the 'gay lifestyle' have destroyed trust. As late as July 2009, incredibly, the then Archbishop of Canterbury was still talking officially about gay partnerships in conventionally homophobic terms: 'whatever the human respect and pastoral sensitivity such persons must be given, their chosen lifestyle is not one that the Church's teaching sanctions'.[5]

Any objection to foolish and unscientific stigmatisation has sometimes been taken as evidence that gays really were the awkward squad. At the same time those who subjected them to homophobic logic and language claimed theological privilege for it. It may be a sign that growing general social disapproval was beginning to get to some conservatives when they went on to claim they were being 'demonised' by anyone who disagreed with them. Such reactions achieve nothing. They fall down because, in fact, it is homophobia that is a lifestyle choice, not homosexuality.

In practice, one-sided reciprocity destroys trust and reinforces inequality. It paralyses any effective dialogue in the Church about homosexuality. Basic respect for the integrity of the other person, whatever their sexual orientation and experience, is necessary for progress in this deeply personal area of life.[6] This includes, of course, people with conservative consciences. They have, however, had the whip hand in the Church for five hundred years, and the better they understand the implications of that fact, the more easily they can be heard.

While gay people were finding increasing understanding and acceptance in Britain, views of sex and marriage in general were developing radically. In its middle years marriage had been seen as a licence for sex. Consent to marriage was a formal green light to any sexual behaviour. Until the very end of the century this included much domestic violence, which police and judges tended to dismiss as 'domestics'. Amazingly, marital rape was only legally recognised in 1991.

Marriage was also the gateway into adult life. Increasingly it has come to be seen as not so much the base camp as the summit of the mountain. In the early twenty-first century most people marry far later than their grandparents did, to seal and not to form permanent relationships.

The increasing complexity of life, and technology's impact, have driven a revolution in social attitudes. Once safe contraception was freely available to women, the automatic link between sex and reproduction was broken. Power over reproduction passed from men to women. Unfolding understanding and clinical practice in relation to transgender people threw up additional moral conundrums.

When, for example, someone has had sex reassignment surgery how should this impact any pre-existing heterosexual marriage? The other spouse may well take the view that it was the person they married not their gender. They may sense a moral duty to fulfil their vows, 'for better for worse … till death us do part'. Hitherto, staying married has been legally impossible. How would a wise pastor advise such a couple in these circumstances? Whatever the answer, the question itself pushes the envelope beyond conventional lines. Make what they will of same-sex marriage, clergy need to think through this subject with new rigour if they are to minister credibly.

One major underlying issue in debates about homosexuality is not the Bible itself, but the way people do their theology. Sometimes those who advocate change are told 'pastorally, of course, you are right, but your theology is lousy'. This reaction says something very interesting about the ways people split their theology from their pastoral practice.

One basic philosophical question asks, 'Does God command what is good, or, starting at the other end, is it his command that makes behaviour good?' Approaching the question deductively, we define what is good in the abstract. Pastoral theology then becomes a matter of applying this good, enforcing it as virtue on real people.

Jesus' way of doing theology was far more inductive. Confronted with a question about the rightness of healing on the Sabbath he did not launch into a complex philosophical investigation of the fourth commandment's meaning. Rather, he appealed to the common conscience by asking how they would treat their child, donkey or ox if it fell in a ditch on a Saturday, then telling them to go figure (Luke 14:5). This response stands alongside his emphatic teaching that the Sabbath was made for people not people for the Sabbath (Mark 2:27). Its moral logic is inductive rather than deductive, like Jesus' statement that a tree is known by its fruit (Matthew 12:33/Luke 6:44).

Deductive theologians start with theory based on their understanding of Scripture and tradition, using that to decide how things should work out in practice. Practical theologians start with reality on the streets, and then use the Bible, tradition and reason to frame an understanding of it. The result largely depends on which end they started from.

The inductive approach could be seen as lax, even undermining received morality. It cannot be dismissed altogether, however, in the light of Jesus' parable of the Good Samaritan. Here, the priest and the Levite's higher thoughts absolved them from paying attention to the rags in the road. The result of their inattention was to disqualify them from fulfilling the greater obligation to a man who could have been their neighbour, but was left for road kill instead.

The question 'Can gay people marry?' can be engaged with in many different theological modes, and on many levels. People tend to produce different answers to it, depending on whether their theology starts at the theoretical or the sharp end.

Western Christians have increasingly, in the past hundred years, focused their theologies on incarnation and spirit rather than abstract principles. The war poet Wilfred Owen encountered Holy Week veneration of the cross in France in 1912. He observed closely the dogmatic and sentimental motives of fellow worshippers, then decided to overcome his Protestant prejudices and join in the liturgy, but for humanistic not dogmatic reasons:

> ... I, too, knelt before that acolyte.
> Above the crucifix I bent my head:
> The Christ was thin, and cold, and very dead:
> And yet I bowed, yea, kissed – my lips did cling.
> (I kissed the warm live hand that held the thing.) [7]

One longstanding English approach to theology could be termed 'holy pragmatic with compassionate realistic ethics.' Theology done in an incarnational mode can never be satisfied with simply enforcing abstract principles, especially when they yield bitter fruit. The jobsworth traffic warden's excuse, 'I don't make the rules', cannot justify cruelty in God's name.

Pastoral theology is the wellspring of Christian doctrine, not its antithesis. Put another way, no Christian can use mere theology to out-pastor the Good Shepherd. We need to find some way of squaring the circle between theory and practice, aligning basic principles of justice, mercy and walking humbly with our God with the ways we treat real people and the effects these have upon them.

In this spirit, any Christian attempt to answer the question honestly has to begin by taking seriously the realities of creation – the facts of life.

Unnatural?

Biology describes what it means to be alive. There are many ideal images of humanity, but the way real people are made will out in the end every time. Bishop Joseph Butler said in 1726: 'Things and Actions are what they are, and the consequences of them will be what they will be: why then should we desire to be deceived?'[1]

What implications does human biology have for our visions of humanity in relation to God?

Ancient Gnostic religions rejected the world as it was. It was nothing to do with God. They saw the order of nature as spiritually inferior to the world of the Spirit. Their philosophers wrote down the visible world as the lower derivative of a whole series of creations. Daily reality was simply evil, and all flesh was evil, or at best an offence and irrelevance to spiritual life.

Christians took a very different line. They took flesh seriously, because God had taken flesh in Jesus in order to redeem the world. According to the logic of the incarnation, humanity and divinity belonged together. St Paul awaited redemption, not *from* the body but *of* the body (Romans 8:23). Surprisingly perhaps, the most difficult part of the faith in the early Church was not believing Jesus was divine, but that he had truly come in the flesh (1 John 4:2–3).

Christian doctrine begins with creation. The book of Genesis said that God saw all he had made, and it was good. Accordingly, there was much to be learnt about God from studying his creation. Modern science began in medieval monasteries and their spin-off universities. God was believed to have laid down natural laws, which were worth studying in themselves. When the Cavendish Laboratory for Experimental Physics opened its doors at Cambridge in 1874 an inscription from Psalm 111:2 went over them: 'The works of the Lord are great, sought out of all them that have pleasure therein.'

St Paul, Pharisee of the Pharisees, looked to Scripture more than nature. In his letter to the Romans, however, he invited his readers to examine the natural world for evidence of God's hand. He illustrated his teaching about resurrection bodies with an example from the natural world – the different kinds of flesh to be found in different animals (1 Corinthians 15:39). He pictured the whole creation groaning in travail like a pregnant woman, awaiting redemption, including the redemption of the body (Romans 8:23).

St Paul disapproved of 'unnatural' practices like men growing their hair, or women cutting it (1 Corinthians 11:14–15). In Romans 1 he laid into idolaters who had given up desire for the opposite sex for 'unnatural' affections. 'Natural' was not the acme of virtue, though. It did not carry all the weight modern people attribute to it, with a far more developed post-Romantic view of nature. God himself could act 'against nature' by grafting wild olives onto cultivated stock (Romans 11:24). Paul's ideas about nature were undeveloped compared even to those of the Middle Ages, but it mattered to him. It had its own tale to tell about the Creator in whom all people live and move and have their being.

Fast-forward 1200 years, and the Italian friar Thomas Aquinas was writing what came to seem a definitive natural theology. Nature was not evil, or random, or some terrible accident. It was as it was because God willed it to be so. He had created the human race in his image. Valuable information about God's character and purposes could be discerned from his workmanship. By following its logic and discerning its purposes, goodness and truth could be discerned.

Thomas's comprehensive natural theology, which shaped Western Christian thinking about sex for almost 800 years, is now wearing thin. A church that sets it in concrete as the rule for today is likely to find itself at serious odds with its members. Thomas's system cannot be the last word because its underlying understanding of nature was very much a child of its time.

Popular ideas of what is natural have changed with the ages in every area of life. For example, the idea of women running competitively was thought to be flagrantly unnatural in late Victorian Europe. Baron Pierre de Coubertin, founder of the modern Olympic Games, banned female athletes from his first Olympiad in 1896 because, he said, allowing them to compete would be 'impractical, uninteresting, unaesthetic, and incorrect'. In 1928, at Amsterdam, female runners first competed, but when a few of them collapsed at the finishing line of the 800-metre race, it was taken as conclusive evidence that their bodies were not made for such exertions. Future women's Olympic races were limited to 400 metres. This decision stood until 1960. Marathons were unthinkable. People shuddered to think of the awful damage running 26 miles would do to female reproductive machinery. When Kathy Switzer ran undercover in the 1967 Boston Marathon she was roughly manhandled off the course by a large man shouting 'Get the hell out of my race and give me those numbers'. The first Olympic women's marathon was held in 1984.

Popular notions of what is natural or unnatural in every part of life are fluid. Almost the only constant about them is change. The terms seem precise and significant. They assume what everyone knows in a given time and place. They are, in fact, entirely bound to the culture of the day. We need to be very wary of turning the terms into moral absolutes.

Thomas drew his understanding of sex from far antiquity. Eight hundred years ago, like other educated people of his age, he turned for his understanding of how the body works to ancient authors, especially Aristotle. The pre-scientific speculations he found there will strike modern readers as comical, but in the thirteenth century they were the best he had.

It was believed, for example, that women were incomplete men, because their sexual organs were on the inside. Their brains were actually conceived as their hearts – brains were thought to be no more than cooling fins, probably because they were so crinkly. Women were constitutionally incapable of exercising command, because when they were conceived the sperm had been too cold. Therefore, obviously, women could not naturally exercise leadership over men.

Thomas assumed, as many still do, that human beings were simply male or female in a crude mutually exclusive way. People were 100 per cent one or the other. Starting with this observation, he wondered why God made sex. Like the fourteenth-century friar he was, he did not particularly rate the 'touchy-feely' aspect of relationships. He saw pleasure as no more than a mean, primal phenomenon, because animals, further down the chain of being, seemed to be capable of it too.

Sex was another behaviour to be found in brute beasts with no understanding. Why did humans have to do it? How could it be ennobled? Human sexuality must have some higher divine purpose. This could be found, he thought, by examining its ends. As sex extends the species, a good thing, Thomas decided its most sublime purpose was reproduction. This is the basis on which some Churches resisted contraception as evil – an unnatural attempt to frustrate the purpose for which God made sex in the first place.

Darwin's work encouraged the notion that sex was primarily about making babies. It was the basic engine of natural selection. In crude evolutionary terms, anything that produces the next generation was good, and anything that didn't flew in the face of basic biological drives, depriving natural selection of its future raw material.

This made homosexuality, potentially, a sin against Darwin as well as God, an abnormality, disorder and aberration from the order of nature. Back in the 1880s, homosexuals were called 'inverts' or 'perverts'. Almost everyone in Britain born before the 1970s grew up breathing in the idea that gayness was profoundly unnatural.

Decriminalised as recently as 1967 in England, 1980 in Scotland, 1982 in Northern Ireland, it drew sniggering on the stage, punishment in the classroom or parade ground, along with blackmail and the occasional suicide. Gay people were scorned, derided and stigmatised on every side. Hospitals devoted serious attention to straightening out gay people by means which seem bizarre now – chemical castration, aversion therapy and intensive counselling.

Throughout the 1970s attitudes softened, but most thoughtful people still saw homosexuality as a disability or illness, if not a crime or sin. Harsh Victorian labels for 'inverts' or 'perverts' fell into disuse, but few doubted that gayness was, objectively speaking, an abnormality.[2]

Freud's work was taken deadly seriously. There might be precious little corroborating evidence for his fascinating theories, but they seemed to explain the inexplicable.

Thus, the 1970s' received wisdom for caring professionals was that homosexuality was an unfortunate emotional disorder arising from the complications of having a distant father and a controlling mother. If a lad didn't form a satisfactory relationship with his own dad he would sooner or later form one with another man. Kinsey's famous survey indicated that a significant proportion of the population had some gay experience. No one, however, undertook the gargantuan task of discovering whether 6 million people in Britain did, indeed, all have particularly distant fathers and dictatorial mothers. So there the subject rested, like all of Freud's theories, as a matter of conjecture.

Curiously, lesbians were almost invisible. Earnest Freudians encountered at parties suggested gay females were all jealous of their fathers for having penises. They were getting their own back, avenging their perceived castration, by taking female partners. Very few, if any, lesbians were aware of ever having wanted a penis in the first place. Such hard evidence of repression clinched the matter.

The past 60 years have seen a revolution in our understanding of life sciences. Amid tens of thousands of research papers no single piece of evidence is uncontested, but a solid picture has emerged of how we are made sexually. In broad terms, the science is pretty much nailed. Research about homosexuality has largely centred on the basic question of its causes – are they matters of nature or nurture?

A larger and more complex view of sexual difference has emerged from research. In the 1950s children learned their biology from 'Janet and John' books. Janet was a girl and John was a boy, and that was all there was to it. Janet was not at all boyish, unless she was a tomboy, but that was entirely an acquired personality. John contained no girlishness, and if he turned out to be more interested in music and art than guns and aeroplanes, he had an artistic temperament that could be contained, as long as it did not run riot.

A very small proportion of babies, however, exhibited uncertain sexual differentiation. From the 1960s the practice of the British National Health Service was to sort them out as soon as possible after birth. Growing up with ambiguity about gender was deemed a horrible fate, and surgery would settle the matter. Where the gonads led, the heart would follow.

Thus, a doctor would examine indeterminate babies' genitals on the first day of their lives, then assign them a sexual category according to their wit, skill, luck and judgement. Surgery followed. Sometimes it worked, and sometimes it did not. On the few occasions it worked, everyone lived happily ever after. Some babies, however, grew up with a disturbing emergent sense of being trapped in the wrong kind of body – exactly the horrible scenario from which surgery had been intended to save them in the first place.

Experience indicated that sexing the species was more complicated with real people than for Janet and John. In the second half of the twentieth century, biology better accounted for the non-binary nature of sexual differentiation, evidence of which could be found in the distant past. Anne Fausto-Sterling reports a curious incident from Piedra, Italy, in 1601:

> A young soldier named Daniel Burghammer shocked his regiment when he gave birth to a healthy baby girl. After his alarmed wife called in his army captain, he confessed to being half male and half female. Christened as a male, he had served as a soldier for seven years while also a practicing blacksmith. The baby's father, Burghammer said, was a Spanish soldier. Uncertain of what to do, the captain called in Church authorities, who decided to go ahead and christen the baby, whom they named Elizabeth. After she was weaned – Burghammer nursed the child with his female breast – several towns competed for the right to adopt her. The Church declared the child's birth a miracle, but granted Burghammmmer's wife a divorce, suggesting that it found Burghammer's ability to give birth incompatible with role of husband.[3]

Jesus in St Matthew's gospel had observed, using the categories and terminology current for his hearers:

> there are eunuchs who have been so from birth, and there are eunuchs who have been made eunuchs by others, and there are eunuchs who have made themselves eunuchs for the sake of the kingdom of heaven. Let anyone accept this who can.
>
> (Matthew 19:12)

The way people are made sexually is not, then, a matter of simple binary switchgear. It is best described by placing any individual at particular points on four different scales. No one of these is entirely given or acquired – nature and nurture have different roles to play in each aspect of the sexual make-up of each one of us.

The first scale is biological sex. Imagine you are a pathologist examining a body that has been found in the river. You cannot ask the person whose body it is what sex they considered themselves to be, nor do you have the evidence of clothing or any other means of identity. How would you determine their biological sex? How many indicators might there be? And if you had to get it right first time what would the most reliable one be?

The answers would surprise Janet and John. If they had time to check all physical indications of sex there would be many, from the form of the body's genitals to the width of linkage between the two halves of the brain.[4] No single indicator would be 100 per cent accurate, and all of them would not indicate one way or the other. All bodies of one sex bear some characteristics of the other.

You could conclude, however, that what you were examining was entirely the product of nature not nurture. In fact even this understandable assumption would be slightly false. The body would bear various physical characteristics arising from the circumstances of its owner's life – scar tissue from a fall or a liver damaged by alcohol, for example.

So, reading the basic physical indicators of sex, people are not crudely male or female but some of each, and usually overwhelmingly one or the other. This is the way they are made; it is then acted on by the chances of life, including nurture. A pathologist with this understanding of what is going on will probably read a body differently from their medieval counterpart. They would want to scan what it was and account for where it had been, rather than trying to speculate about the purpose for which its various parts might have been created.

It is not easy to define the purpose of any body part exhaustively. Nearly all human beings have two legs. You could say they were designed for walking, and any other use was unnatural. Some people are unable to walk on their legs, and others may choose not to at different times, but this does not make them less than fully human, or constitute a sin. A body might belong to a circus clown whose job was to walk on their hands. It might belong to a disabled athlete who was unable to walk but a skilled player of wheelchair football. It would be largely pointless to interpret the body in terms of some notional ideal of what 'natural' use its parts might have. Any part can do anything of which it is capable, without necessarily committing a sin or contradicting a creation purpose. Indeed, the more purposes it can fulfil, the more wonderful it might be considered.

Having established the extent to which any individual has a male or female biological sex, the question arises, 'How do they relate sexually to others?' or 'To whom are they attracted?' This is a second dimension of sexuality, 'sexual orientation'. Back in the 1940s Alfred Kinsey suggested there were six points on a scale between exclusively homosexual and exclusively heterosexual. The great majority of the population would usually place themselves towards the heterosexual end. It's interesting to note not only where they would be, but also how much variation there might be at different times in their lives about where they thought they belonged.

For most people their position would be fairly fixed, but for a smaller minority of males and a larger proportion of females, there would be a significant degree of fluidity about their sexual orientation. There are some intriguing correlations between sexuality and other human distinctive characteristics. For example, 30 per cent of the autism community are LGBTQI.[5] This correlation needs to be taken into account if Churches are to do as they usually claim they want to and welcome all equally. Its whys and wherefores remain to be researched, let alone understood.

Bisexual people would place differently on the orientation scale at different times. Pansexual people would place all over it. Around 1 per cent of the population could be described as asexual, consistently low on any scale of attraction. Sexual orientation seems at first sight to be a basic given, but some people show a significant degree of fluidity about it.

This phenomenon has been well tested in the field by the experience of various attempts by Evangelical organisations to change sexual orientation. These have almost universally failed. This kind of endeavour seems to have caused far more harm than good to those who engaged in it. An interesting but tiny minority, however, have claimed that their sexual orientations were actually changed in this way. Experimentation in this area, while generally hazardous and radically unlikely to yield a successful result, can very occasionally significantly alter the lives of a very few, generally bisexual, people.

How far is sexual orientation given and how far acquired? It seems to be largely a matter of nature, but not entirely. In no particular individual is it primarily a matter of choice, except perhaps for bisexual people and, perhaps, asexual people, although these last would be most unlikely to be able to do very much about any choice they made.

The safest general picture of sexual orientation consistent with science is well articulated by Wendy Lawson:

> Having an orientation that is not heterosexual but homosexual is just as moral and as important as being heterosexual. I believe that it too is part of nature's design and overall plan to protect and enhance the diversity of the human species.[6]

So far, all we have considered are mainly physical phenomena of sex and sexual orientation. How do people understand and express themselves sexually? This brings in a third dimension of sexuality, gender identity – a person's sense of gender. From an anthropological perspective, all societies have gender categories that form a social identity for their members in relation to those around them, especially as they grow up.

The psychological evidence is that gender identity is usually established by the end of the toddler stage of development, and can very seldom be changed after that. It seems most three-year-olds will be able to identify themselves as boy or girl, although they will not yet grasp everything that means. In the 1970s there was quite a fashion for parents to bring up their boys to play with dolls not guns, but this approach was seldom wildly successful.

A small number of people experience what is called gender identity dysphoria. The terminology describes a real phenomenon, but must not be used in a way that suggests that what is actually a gender variation is some kind of illness. The 'dysphoria' describes the unease experienced, not the condition giving rise to it. Its characteristic sign is a feeling, strengthening as life goes on, that they are of one gender but living in the body of a different sex. Transgender people can receive gender reassignment treatments.

Nature or nurture apply differently to different aspects of gender identity. On the one hand the behaviours and attitudes that define it are acquired, a matter of nurture. On the other, people's sense of maleness or femaleness is largely defined by the society within which they grow up and is handed down to them 'off the peg'. For the vast majority of people their gender identity is very difficult to change once established.

Gender identity is largely a matter of the mind, but it gives rise to behaviours which help define people's sexuality. This is a fourth dimension of sexuality, gender expression.

There are many different ways of expressing masculinity or femininity in any society. Anthropologically tuned signals evoke responses in others around a person, and from this constant social dialogue each person develops their own way of expressing who they are sexually. This in turn helps other people formulate their sense of what kinds of behaviour express gender. People used to talk in a rather crude and basic way about 'sex acts' as though the scope of sexuality was exhausted by a list of behaviours. It made sexuality a kind of X-factor that kicked in on the way to bed, that could only be described using euphemisms like 'homosexual genital acts'. This terminology is vague, stupid and inadequate. It implies that only particular things people do have a sexual dimension to them. It would be far more accurate to see all behaviour as having a sexual dimension to some degree.

Euphemisms about homosexuality are often confusing and vague. They break down when expressed in anger. Angry letters are penned to supporters of gay rights, denouncing them for trying to be kind but 'encouraging buggery'. The last word is written in large capital letters, underlined with stabbing motions until it goes through the paper.

Evidence is, however, that the majority of gay people do not engage in anal sex, while a significant proportion of straight couples do.[7] It is important that any position the Church may take on the subject acknowledges this fact. Personal intimacy is almost impossible to analyse objectively, but indications are that anal sex is, in fact, practised by some 30 per cent of gay couples. The proportion of straight couples who practise it seems to be very similar. Given that around 2 per cent of the male population self-identify as gay, it could be guessed that anal sex is practised by some 17 million people in Britain, of whom, perhaps, around one and a half million would place significantly on a gay scale. Allowing the wrongness of anal sex, those who wish to suppress it would do far better to focus their energies on the 85 per cent of those who practise it who are not gay than to make it the defining characteristic of gay people in order to try and stir up disgust against them.

If Church officials really are expected to appoint themselves inquisitors of bedroom behaviour, they need to be clear about exactly what they have in mind.

What is 'practising' homosexuality? Holding hands? Sitting on the sofa together watching TV like *The Simpsons*? Or what? Unless people are prepared to be more specific about exactly which sexual behaviours require correction, and apply their rules equally to gay and straight people, it is hard to see a basis here for decisions that will stand up to judicial review.

In some ways, gender expression is the most obvious dimension of sexuality to locate within the realm of nurture. That said, like gender identity it is formed of habits first expressed and reinforced by surrounding culture. Daily personal habits become deeply ingrained, and it would be wrong to think that just because they are socially acquired this makes them readily changeable.

It is understandable for moralists to want to know whether the way we are made sexually is given or acquired. People can hardly be held morally responsible for the way they are made. People increasingly do not believe homosexuality is harmful, sinful or shameful. They believe it is a phenomenon within nature rather than an offence against it. If this is all it is, the extent to which it is a matter of nature or nurture carries no particular moral significance.

There remain, however, deeper questions of natural theology. How are aspects of the character of God written on the body? What can we learn about his creation purpose from the ways we are made? Late-twentieth-century biology, with all its diversity and complexity, makes the simplistic 'Janet and John' view of sex seem inadequate. Thomas Aquinas approached nature to search the works of God and learn from the creation something more of the Creator. The sexual dimension of the way we are made is very diverse, sometimes ambiguous, and deeply personal.

Of course, contemporary science is not definitive. In a very few years anything said now may appear hopelessly outdated. A future return to the anthropology of the thirteenth century is very unlikely. What sexual anthropology might come from following a similar path to Thomas's today, but based on our understanding, not his pre-scientific one? What does it mean now, morally, to be created as a sexual being? And as Thomas might ask were he alive today, what is the creation purpose of the way in which people are formed? How does any individual's sexual make-up fit into the whole purpose of creation?

'The glory of God', said the early Christian bishop Irenaeus of Lyons, 'is a living human and human life is the vision of God.'[8] The Psalmist says God, who knew people in the womb, has knit them together 'fearfully and wonderfully' (Psalm 139:14). Presumably the Lord knew what he was doing when he ordered nature as he did. If he had intended to make people male or female in a binary 'Janet and John' way he could have done so, but he chose not to. How come there is such a degree of ambiguity and greyscale about every aspect of sexual formation?

Trying to answer this question leads into the new and developing area of study, epigenetics. People often assume that genes are simply predictive indicators. If someone has a dominant red-haired gene they will have red hair. What could be simpler? This approach has driven the search for a single 'gay gene'. Some have wondered if a single genetic marker would turn out to be entirely indicative of sexual orientation.

The search for the gay gene has turned into a wild goose chase. Identical twin studies indicate a massively increased chance of identical twins both being gay. Any human body amounts to a particular permutation of a wide variety of potentials, including sexual ones. The body is a genetic cocktail, containing no single ingredient that can be labelled as a gay gene. Individual genes are switched on or off in relation to other genes by an elaborate interfacing process driven by hormones in the womb. The study of this process – epigenetics – tracks the way in which particular permutations occur.

Thomas Aquinas looked to the purpose of body parts to understand their meaning within creation. When a baby is formed nature has two crucial and very different purposes.

One is to plot a critical path through the possibilities laid down in the available genetic material that will produce a viable human being. The other is to transmit to the next generation but one a maximum number of options from which its bodies can be permutated. It becomes desirable for each generation to privilege a range of sexual and reproductive characteristics, over and above hell-for-leather maximisation of breeding.

The depth and subtlety of this process not only reflects the nature of creation, shot through as it is with seemingly infinite diversity and complexity. It also helps to prevent future overpopulation. A modern Thomas could interpret the nature of sexuality somewhat like this: The God of diversity creates far more than mere breeding machines – a world of variety, delight and seemingly infinite possibilities.

Medieval natural theology was obsessively anxious to locate the meaning of sex in its aim, reproduction. This tends to instrumentalise the body, reducing it to a sexual breeding appliance. Marriage becomes 'sacramentalised propagation of the species'. Homosexuality is reduced to a hedonistic desire to commit sinful acts. All such reductionism is morally suspect, because it leaves out the personal and spiritual dimensions of the matter. Moral responsibility is based on how people use their free will. It is morally more responsible to see the body as a subject, a potential temple of the Spirit, than an object whose highest purpose is no more than reproduction.

Contemporary human biology implies that everyone is served up a particular genetically based combination that develops personally and socially as it acquires attitudes and habits. It follows that nature and nurture are actually opposite ends of the same continuum.

The cause of homosexuality is, in fact, no more than the cause of any sexuality. All human options are equally natural. Any individual's placement on the four scales of sexuality is a part of their human make-up. It should be accepted for what it is, not stigmatised or punished.

The ancient Gnostics thought people could be punished for the way they were, as well as the things they did. Real moral responsibility comes not from the hand nature dealt you but knowledge of good and evil. This is the clear message of the story of the Garden of Eden. It is plain that only a very small aspect of any individual's sexuality is morally negotiable. Most is hardwired, reinforced by society.

Does this mean that any sexual behaviour is morally neutral? By no means. Violent, exploitative, selfish, casual, reckless or other harmful forms of sex are wrong. They are no more or less wrong for LGBTQI people than anyone else, for exactly the same reasons.

The Church of England's 1928 wedding liturgy says that the natural instincts and affections implanted by God need to be hallowed and directed aright. This is difficult if not impossible to do if a culturally despised subset of them are judged to be wrong, simply on the basis of the direction in which they were pointed. Given that human beings are made up in such a complicated, partly changeable and subtle way, the fairest option for society is to permit people with any sexuality to marry anyone else legally, according to their luck, skill and judgement.

People in a society that views homosexuality as a natural phenomenon that occurs throughout creation will apply exactly the same moral requirements to it as to any other sexual behaviour. In this sense, opening marriage to gay people actually raises the moral stakes. Back in the 1950s when gayness itself was abominable and stigmatised it was easy to think that if you were gay that was in itself such a sin that whatever followed was minor. The whole world of cottaging, coded furtiveness, innuendo and duplicity did not promote clear moral understanding, responsibility or discourse.

Once gay relationships are no longer seen as intrinsically disordered, they can be tested by exactly the same moral criteria as others. Do they display virtues of permanence, stability, mutual love and fidelity? Relationships are judged better by their fruit than by their configuration.

Thomas believed homosexuality was an intrinsic moral disorder. He was led to this conclusion by examining the purposes of various body parts and interpreting what he saw by the standards of ancient pre-scientific biology. He concluded that sex was basically a reproductive mechanism and, teleologically speaking, non-procreative sex was wrong. So homosexuality was a profound offence against nature. If people seek the origins of it as an abnormality, that is what they will find. To a certain extent, the answer is locked up in the way the question is asked.

We can undertake a similar process of inquiry today, but using our understanding of biology for raw material. Of course, our understanding of biology is only provisional. That said, we have a considerably clearer and more detailed picture of the processes of creation than was current 800 years ago. It indicates that homosexuality is simply a particular permutation of the possibilities locked up in any human being. Its cause is the same as the cause of heterosexuality. From a theological point of view, it is simply one possible outcome of the way in which God made us all. That fact in itself implies an equality between people of all sexual orientations that would have horrified Queen Victoria.

It is fairly widely accepted among Christian Churches in the West that the time has come to stop stigmatising exceptional people. In theory, all are welcome. The arrival of a gay married couple in some congregations, however, may still cause raised eyebrows. Why do they have to be able to get married? Doesn't this involve redefining marriage? Should this be done? And can it be?

Equality or bust

The facts of life about sex and marriage give rise to social as well as personal phenomena. The way people are made results in many different ways for them to understand themselves in relation to others. Every society that has ever been has had its particular concept of sex and marriage received from its past and developed as it passes from generation to generation. Now people from different cultures move about in ways their ancestors would have found incredible. As they mix and match, cultural development becomes much more complicated and messy than in earlier, more self-contained societies.

No other area of life, perhaps, has been as hedged about by taboo, myth, fantasy, poetry and art as sex. Gender identity and expression have often been seen as to some extent the preserve of religion. The professional guardians of the sacred have taken special responsibility for personal boundaries and transitional rituals.

People fear what they don't fully understand or control more than what they do. An air of mystery, fear and taboo usually attends sexual exploration. Most societies develop concepts of shame to police the boundaries of sexual behaviour. Rules about modesty additionally make the whole subject impossible to talk about without incurring disapproval.

Western marriage throws up a wall of privacy around itself that has often in the past made it difficult to talk about what goes on within it. Homosexuality has been doubly awkward to talk honestly about, within and around marriage.

Christian opponents of the notion that gay people can marry sometimes rubbish other Christians' support for it as mere social conformity. What role does culture have in discerning this question?

One feature of Christianity has been how well it travels across frontiers by being radically open to different cultures. A fundamental text for understanding mission in the second half of the twentieth century has been Vincent Donovan's *Christianity Rediscovered*.[1] This describes his mission, as a Roman Catholic Holy Ghost Father, to grow faith among the Maasai people of East Africa in an authentic organic way, rather than imposing it on them. All mission that is not imperialistic receives freely from the milieu within which it works, freely but not uncritically. It transposes itself into new modes, and, as it finds and makes a home in each new culture, baptises it. Doing this enriches as well as grows the worldwide Church.

The question of how the Church relates to culture is crucial to this aspect of Christianity. In 1951 the American theologian Richard Niebuhr published his book *Christ and Culture*.[2] He outlined five different viewpoints Christians could take to society around them. Exclusive Christians define Christ *against* culture. What he called cultural Christians see history as an emerging tale of grace acting on nature to produce a 'Christ *of* culture'. Others define 'Christ *above* culture' – the sum total of all the syntheses of history. Dualists would see Christ *and* culture in a paradoxical relationship where faith struggles against unbelief throughout history. The most sophisticated and empathetic line, he suggested, was perhaps the most popular aspirational one, Christ *transforming* culture from within. This kind of Christianity is a social and spiritual process to transform the world in the present moment rather than defining origins or awaiting the apocalypse.

Niebuhr's framework yields models to help understand different Christian reactions to living in particular cultures. History, however, is not fixed. It develops. A progressive attitude in 1900 would seem very retro a hundred years later. Christians can easily use Niebuhr to sanctify their own cultural proclivities.

Everything about his categories, however, is subjective, time-bound and relative.

There is an old joke about a bishop who wished to inspire a squad of Edwardian Boy Scouts to be bolder Christians. He told them a story about a boy at scout camp who, when all the other boys were reading in bed before lights out, knelt to say his prayers at the foot of his bed. 'Now, boys,' said the bishop, 'can you imagine anything braver than that?' An awed silence was broken by the youngest scout saying, 'I think I can, Sir. It was the Lambeth Conference and at bedtime all the bishops were kneeling down by their beds saying their prayers except for one who lay in bed reading a detective novel. I think that must have been jolly brave.'

Resistance to gay people marrying could be thought heroically countercultural in some Western contexts, but it would be drearily conformist in contemporary Nigeria or Edwardian Britain. Niebuhr's categories can be applied to any theological position in any society. So what? There is so much variety among human cultures that even if it were possible to fix the categories accurately through the ages, they would reveal almost nothing about the subject itself. If we want to discern the truth of any subject, best leave Niebuhr out of it until its rights and wrongs have been established on other grounds.

Increasingly since the 1990s, Christian resistance to gay people being allowed to marry has centred on big assertions about the definition of marriage.

This rhetoric seems to have been born among the US moral majority in the late twentieth century as they saw the prospect of same-sex marriage drawing closer. The phrase enabled Christians to acknowledge the existence of gay people, but simultaneously rubbish any possibility of them marrying. It depersonalised the issue by reducing it to a notional theoretical level. Christians could affirm the nice lesbian couple next door while reducing any hope the pair might have of marrying to a philosophical misunderstanding with potentially serious social consequences.

Humans do not make divine or logical rules, so Christians could not be held responsible for the impact of their viewpoint on the human beings involved.

This redefinition argument has been argued forcefully before church synods, parliaments and debating chambers all over the world. Theoretically it seems extremely powerful, and those who fear and resist same-sex marriage at a gut level have certainly seen it as their killer argument. It's most effective when preaching to the choir. It has, puzzlingly perhaps to its proponents, cut almost no ice with anyone else.

Truth to tell, non-homophobes often find redefinition rhetoric absurd. Marriage has in fact been radically and continuously redefined down the ages by the lived experience of married people. Most couplings have been polygamous, but many geometries exist. Various examples of same-sex marriage, right or wrong, are to be found in the anthropological annals of Africa, China and Europe. At least two Roman emperors were in same-sex marriages before the practice was banned by the Theodosian Code in AD 342.[3] The definition of marriage has never been fixed, including its gender aspects.

Portentous assertions that monogamy between a man and a woman has been the anthropological gold standard from the dawn of time are simply false. Marriage everywhere has always been continuously redefined, occasionally radically, by the lived experience of married people, reflected in their custom and law.

There are at least two other basic reasons that redefinition rhetoric about same-sex marriage only seems to convince those who oppose it.

First and foremost, the argument is about words. A bully was an admirable person in the sixteenth century, but not 400 years later, because the word had fundamentally changed in meaning. Biologists used the word 'heterosexual' as recently as 1963 to mean 'pertaining to, characteristic of both sexes', rather than 'pertaining to sexual relations between people of the opposite sex'.[4] Meanwhile the meaning that has become customary today was developing on another track.

The English language is like that. *The Oxford English Dictionary* was founded on historical principles, to describe a living language. Across the English Channel, the long-standing efforts of the Academie Française to police language and eliminate 'Franglais' have been sterile and largely fruitless. There is no similar enforcement body in the English-speaking world.

Anyway, protesters against the redefinition of marriage would have to be careful when calling in the Word Police, if they existed. *The Oxford English Dictionary's* primary definition of 'marriage', current since 1297, would be perfectly usable for a same-sex marriage.[5]

The fact is, asserting that a particular definition is unchangeable does not make it so. All concepts and definitions are provisional. One person's unthinkable change may well be another's timely reform. Living institutions continuously develop, as do the rules for human relationships. They always have and they always will. A simple demand that any meaning be set in concrete is only appealing to people who do not want a particular change.

Gay people marry for the same reasons as anyone else, not in order to doctor the dictionary. Some of their lived relationships have long been indistinguishable from heterosexual marriages, and it was this fact that led many, including, eventually, most UK legislators, to draw the obvious conclusion.

Before civil partnerships were invented conservative critics warned they would soon be seen as marriages. This is exactly what has happened. It probably will not comfort anti-homosexual culture warriors to have called the issue correctly. As the number of married gay couples increases, they will themselves become yet more evidence that same-sex marriage is possible.

Redefinition arguments have proved powerless against what is sometimes called the 'duck' proposition – if it looks like a duck, flies like a duck, walks like a duck and quacks like a duck, it probably is a duck. People have now seen gay friends marry and this has drained credibility from the idea that such a thing is impossible.

A second reason that redefinition rhetoric fails is that it has usually come backed by dire warnings about the damage same-sex marriages will do to society. It is hard to speculate what this damage might be. Suggestions have included the damage that follows once people are confused and abandon the old 'Janet-and-John' binarism about gender. As we have seen, this is, biologically, a mirage, so whether gay people marry or not, everyone will just have to learn to live without it anyway. Desperate attempts to come up with some notional damage same-sex marriage would do to heterosexual unions did not convince anyone except those who needed no convincing.

What actually happened in countries that allowed gay people to marry is less than sensational. A small number of gay people got married, and life carried on. A substantial minority of the population continue to believe, as they are entitled to, that marriage should be, or can only be, between a man and a woman. These people's needs are easily met in full, not by consigning gay people to second-class relationships but by refraining from marrying someone of the same sex. Doing this does not require legislation or even self-control from heterosexuals.

The strongest form of redefinition argument claims that it is simply impossible for gay people to marry. If difference of sex is an essential part of the definition of marriage, of course, it can't be done. This arguable debating proposition begins to crumble once people start doing the allegedly impossible. Some people believe that those who have not married in a particular Church are not really married. They are welcome to their views. In a liberal democracy no one will be persecuted for them. It would, however, be as irrational for families or employers who really believe same-sex marriage is impossible to take action against others who entered such unions as it would be to ban them from keeping unicorns.

The arrival of legally married same-sex couples could be a good time to say farewell to one old friend from the debates that led to change, the term 'gay marriage'. If it is wrong to label people with terms they do not own, this terminology is unusable. Father Andrew Foreshew-Cain, the first Church of England gay incumbent to marry a same-sex partner, describes a well-intentioned church meeting at which it was much used:

> It is a phrase that irritates me intensely. So I said that as someone about to marry I was not getting 'gay-married', nor did I ask my fiancé to 'gay-marry' me when we got engaged. At the wedding of two young women last month there was never any mention of them getting 'lesbian married' or it being a 'lesbian wedding'. I am getting married, they got married. Marriage is marriage – for a gay couple, a lesbian couple and even those few straight couples who bother these days. I asked if people could simply stop bracketing some relationships with a codicil as if they were in some sense 'other'. I was polite and open about how uncomfortable I was feeling. No one took any notice. 'Gay marriage' remained the phrase of the evening.

> So, straight people, from now on I am going to talk about 'heterosexual marriage' whenever the marriage of straight people comes up. And for those of us who are blessed to have loving partners of the same gender – marriage is the order of the day. See how the straights like your principal relationship and commitment being set apart with an identifying descriptive every time. (And if I ever hear another unconscious slip into a discussion of paedophilia when marriage is being discussed I am going to ask every straight male person I meet about rape.) [6]

The progressive Catholic journalist Mary Elizabeth Williams also finds the phrase insulting:

as we recognise that two men or two women can forge
together loving, enduring, legally recognised unions, it's
time to retire the belittling phrase 'gay marriage' itself,
once and for all. Calling it 'gay marriage' is like calling it
'black marriage' or 'geriatric marriage' or any other absurd,
insulting modifier. It anoints the institution with otherness
and makes it seem outside the norm. Marriage Substitute.
Marriage Lite. I Can't Believe It's Not Marriage![7]

Many Christians who believe homosexuality is sinful have
developed a particular approach to gay people that asserts they
are affirming the person while abominating their behaviour.
They follow this with a rider that they are not judging or being
homophobic, which invites the response that it is really for those
on the sharp end of their attitude to decide that. Many Christian
denominations have adopted similar arguments to square the
circle between homophobic theology and compassionate
pastoral practice. The idea is rather like a road sign once seen in
India that proclaimed 'we love you, but not your rash driving'.

This approach contains at least three basic flaws. It can never
be more than a well-intentioned halfway house towards real
understanding and acceptance.

Firstly, 'love the sinner, hate the sin' carries within it the
assumption that homosexuality is in itself a sin. It pathologises
an aspect of who people are, then defines them by it. For this
reason it is only ever convincing in a structurally homophobic
society. However stunning their relationships may be, or not,
everyone resents phoney attempts to be nice to them, or to
patronise them, and craves basic acceptance and understanding
of who they are as they are.

Old-fashioned surgeons used to describe patients as cases.
Mrs Jones was 'the arthritic hip in bed 4'. Like all name-calling,
this way of seeing people dehumanises them. When we define
someone in this kind of way the simplicity of the label will
always overpower the complexity and subtlety of the real person

to whom it is applied. Labelling absolves us from understanding the other person as they are.

No matter how politely people are pathologised, turned into an issue, scapegoated simply for being as they are, or otherwise interpreted through the lens of someone else's prejudice, the results will always be woe. The behaviour of those who do these things, however kindly intentioned and polite, inevitably falls short of the standard Jesus set his disciples for their interactions with others.

The Sermon on the Mount charges Jesus' followers to love their neighbours as themselves by doing as they would be done by. God is the judge, not his followers. The Lord's harshest criticism was reserved for the scribes and Pharisees, for their tendency to focus on externals and to strike superior postures in the conceit of their own hearts. Love begins when we receive the other person as they see themselves and as they are.

Love distorted by partiality and prejudice is especially painful and damaging between parents and children.

Claire Jones, an Evangelical Christian feminist who blogs under the title 'The Art of Uncertainty', has written movingly of how her attitude to her mother of 'loving the sinner but hating the sin' was challenged by a film in which gay people spoke for themselves:

> I loved my mum anyway, sure. I assured her as much when she first told me she was gay.
>
> I still love you just the same, Mum.
>
> The 'anyway' was implicit. I love you, even though I don't love that. I love you anyway, because I don't accept the gay thing as part of you. It's not you, really. I love you despite this bit that I refuse to love.

Those are the kinds of words that some of the parents on this film spoke and wrote to their gay kids when they came out. Those words represent the supposedly 'nicer face' of a deep prejudice, expressed in so many nastier ways. Those are the kinds of words that led a young woman to hang herself, as acknowledged by her now repentant mother who had written them.

I know what I would have said, a few years ago. I would have said I was accepting my mum as she truly was, but not acknowledging sin as part of her identity. As if I was doing her a favour. Just like, I'd have said, my true identity is not in the lies I tell or the gossip I spread or the ways I hurt other people. I am not 'Liar' or 'Cheat' or 'Bully' even though I might do those things, so my mum was not 'Gay', whatever life she led.

I can't quite believe how damaging that perspective is. How incredibly damaging to equate one person's deep love for another person with my lies and anger and gossip. How sickening, how vile, to call someone else's love 'sin', to call the very best in them 'evil', to pour shame on the most natural way in which we mirror God, by loving others.

I'm so sorry for the damage I did simply by holding and expressing that view. Those people on that film … they could have been me.

I wish there were stronger words to say it, but I'll make do with the ones I have:

I love Mum.

Not anyway, not despite, not except. I love who she is, and I love how she loves. I love her love for me, for her friends, for her Church, for her partner. I love the way she models to me how to love better. I love how she models Jesus to me.

Of course I don't think Mum's perfect, and I know she'd be the first to stand up and say it. There are things I wish she'd do more, others I wish she'd do less. But I will not, I cannot ever again, say that I wish she loved less. It makes absolutely no sense for someone with faith in a God who is Love to say that a person's love is wrong. The Bible doesn't say it and I won't say it.

I'm convinced that as I'm called to follow Jesus, I'm called to fight prejudice. I'm called to challenge ignorance. I'm called to celebrate love as something holy and beautiful, and to learn from it much more about the God who loves me.

I hope you can forgive me, Mum.[8]

Thomas Merton points out how significant and searching this discipline is:

The beginning of love is the will to let those we love be perfectly themselves, the resolution not to twist them to fit our own image. If in loving them we do not love what they are, but only their potential likeness to ourselves, then we do not love them: we only love the reflection of ourselves we find in them.[9]

Hanging onto a fixed idea of the other person and setting our partial view of them above theirs, then trying to make up for the disrespect involved by being nice about them is not enough. Refusal to take anyone's self-identity seriously, including gay people's, fails; it fails not some liberal principle but the fundamental Christian law of love.

Jane Elliott is a veteran campaigner against racial injustice. An Iowa teacher, she reacted to Martin Luther King's assassination by devising workshops to help students understand and combat racist attitudes in themselves. She divided her class into two groups according to the colour of their eyes. Both groups were marked with coloured sashes and those with brown eyes were encouraged within the exercise to treat those with blue eyes as inferior.

Often, she discovered, blue-eyed liberal students would protest against the methods of the workshop by saying they did not see other people as black but simply as people. This sounds very noble perhaps, but Elliott came to see it as nothing more than a polite form of racism. Every person has characteristics such as sex, race, age and physical stature. An equal and just society does not empty these of meaning, but respects them as they are. Black people do not have to be honorary whites, or even colourless, but who they are as they see themselves.

> You do not have a right to say to a person, 'I do not see you as you are. I want to see you as I would be more comfortable seeing you.'[10]

Failure to realise this basic truth, especially in organisations as invested as many Churches are in niceness, is the final refuge of discriminatory behaviour and attitudes. It enables those who have the whip hand to retain control and see the minority group as the problem. This mechanism has distinctive mantras, 'separate but equal' and 'some of my best friends are ...'. As people confront their prejudices about race and gender there is usually a transitional stage at which they see the problem as belonging to black people or women, who must be humoured and promoted as guests at someone else's party.

Discriminatory attitudes are everyone's problem. The only measure of real progress is equality, and the litmus test for that is interchangeability. A society that tolerates discrimination diminishes itself, not only the people against whom prejudice is directed.

Secondly, there is a fundamental problem about saying you love someone but reserve the right to sit in judgement over them. Jesus calls his disciples to love their neighbour as themselves, on the basis of equality. 'Judge not', he says, 'that ye be not judged.' St Paul reinforces this teaching by asking his readers in Rome to reflect seriously on their tendency to judgementalism: 'Who are you to pass judgment on servants of another? It is before their own lord that they stand or fall' (Romans 14:4).

The 'love the sinner, hate the sin' stance carries a third inadequacy. Anglicans love middle ways, compromise solutions and sitting on the fence. It's a commendable instinct and sometimes very wise. It is only possible, however, if there is, in fact, a fence to sit on. The habit of steering round difficulties rather than facing them dies hard. Acceptance of another human being on their own terms, however, is not something you can half do. You do or you don't. And the accepter is not the arbiter of whether integration has been achieved, but the acceptee. Anything less perpetuates inequality by allowing the person who has the whip hand to retain control of the way the more vulnerable person is being framed.

The fact is, either the blacks can get on the bus or they can't. Saying they can, but making them sit at the back in order to accommodate the prejudices of more retro-minded whites, will not do. It is only a modified form of racism, not a just and equal society. During the debates on equal marriage of 2013 some argued, 'Gays already have civil partnerships. Why do they need marriage?'

The answer is that having your own ghettoised form of something is not the same as having access to the real thing. The Bantu homelands policy during the final stages of apartheid relied on the 'separate but equal' argument, however unequal matters actually were. Since non-whites could have their own homes, townships and even hospitals and universities, there would be no need for them to have access to the white ones. Blacks-only beaches were an integral part of apartheid not the answer to it. Equality demands not sameness but equal access to the same benefits for all.

The all-or-nothing nature of inclusion becomes critical for the military. Either women could serve on ships or they couldn't. Once they were allowed on board, they were on board. Giving them their own ships was not the answer, because it would not deploy people according to their talents, or produce an integrated and effective service.

Furthermore, unlike ecclesiastical contexts, military ones carry high risks. Service personnel rely for their lives on those with whom they serve. They have to see themselves as equal members of a team facing common dangers. Without confidence to do this, the risk to everyone increases. Prejudice costs lives.

It may be that one reason the Church of England has been able to sail around in circles about gays for the past 30 years, listening and listening but hearing nothing, is that establishment bickering about dogma is a low-stakes pastime for the people at the top. Stakes are higher for the gay people under discussion – back to the bacon and eggs joke. The Church is occasionally pictured in Scripture in military terms, imagery that calls for focus and intention beyond the levels Anglicans have hitherto been able to manage with their gay issue.

If Anglican bishops really believe it is impossible for gay people to marry, married gay clergy pose a pastoral conundrum like married transgender people. How would they regularise their position? Divorce? But hang on, they can't have been married in the first place. Separate? But the Church has already said they can live together. The Church's response to such questions needs to be far more explicit, clearer and more coherent than hitherto.

The enactment of same-sex marriage has raised the bar on inclusion, and thus may have done the Church of England a favour. After decades of badging up moral cowardice as theology, it has produced an urgent measurable, with no middle ground, to which church authorities must react. It is the end of 'don't ask, don't tell'. This may not be comfortable, but at least it holds out the hope of a solution at long last.

Same-sex marriage was introduced in England not as an act of libertinism, but simple equality. The 2010 Equality Act had drawn together many years of anti-discrimination legislation into a simple package that protected particular characteristics – age, disability, gender reassignment, marriage and civil partnership, pregnancy and maternity, race, religion and belief, sex and sexual orientation. In principle no one should be discriminated against in work or services on any of these grounds.

Some Christians do not like the thought of equality. They believe divine right is more important, and equality is a human rather than divine virtue. Acknowledging human rights and administering justice require equality, and these concerns are not thought to have anything particular to do with God. As a result, equality is de-emphasised and often denounced as 'secular'.

The God of the Hebrews values equality. He is emphatically no respecter of rank or human status. Equality is a fundamental underlying component of Abrahamic religion. The Hebrew Scriptures teach radical forms of moral responsibility, on the basis of assumed equality. Their prophets rail against excessive economic inequality and oppression. Their law codes proscribe extreme economic or social exploitation. God is just, and loves justice. 'The rich and the poor have this in common: the LORD is the maker of them all' (Proverbs 22:2).

Against this background, Jesus taught his disciples to call no one father, because they had only one father in heaven (Matthew 23:9). St Peter adduces a lesson in equality from his close encounter with non-kosher food on the roof at Joppa: 'I truly understand that God shows no partiality, but in every nation anyone who fears him and does what is right is acceptable to him' (Acts 10:34–35).

St Paul tells the Romans, right up front, that 'God shows no partiality' (Romans 2:11).

The Epistle of James teaches that it is absurd and godless for a Christian assembly to treat people differently depending on their economic status:

> My brothers and sisters, do you with your acts of favouritism really believe in our glorious Lord Jesus Christ? For if a person with gold rings and in fine clothes comes into your assembly, and if a poor person in dirty clothes also comes in, and if you take notice of the one wearing the fine clothes and say, 'Have a seat here, please,' while to the one who is poor you say, 'Stand there,' or, 'Sit at my feet,' have you not made distinctions among yourselves, and become judges with evil thoughts?
>
> (James 2:1–4)

The assembly of the baptised, from the Day of Pentecost, was a company of equals. Jesus had talked of his disciples as equally children of one father:

> You know that among the Gentiles those whom they recognise as their rulers lord it over them, and their great ones are tyrants over them. But it is not so among you; but whoever wishes to become great among you must be your servant, and whoever wishes to be first among you must be slave of all. For the Son of Man came not to be served but to serve, and to give his life as a ransom for many.
>
> (Mark 10:42–5)

St Paul's great picture of the Church as a body says that every part has its distinct task, some parts more publicly honoured than others, but each equally a part of, and valuable to, the whole body (1 Corinthians 12:18–27).

Christianity could not have transcended the tribal and local religions of the ancient Mediterranean without prioritising equality. It spread far and fast because of its radical openness, which gave it the ability to transpose itself into a wide range of cultural milieux, building an equal community that reflected an equal order at the end of time, as envisaged in the book of Revelation.

In practice the primitive ideal of equality was coloured by various hierarchical mindsets from the cultures within which it grew. The net effect, however, of spreading across many cultures was to neutralise the dominance of any particular kind of inequality among disciples. Giving equal worth to others emerged as a Christian virtue. Believers tried to see others as God saw them, equally partakers of the Divine nature in a way that cut across the sociological categories that otherwise defined them restrictively – race, slavery, class and gender.

Equality is the ground bass of the Bible story from the Garden of Eden to the New Jerusalem. It facilitated the expansion of Christianity. The inclusion of religion among the protected categories in the Equality Act 2010 has made it an engine of religious literacy for non-religious civil servants. It is sad if hierarchical habits of mind and fear of equality have made it God's dirty word.

Religious people sometimes lump equality in with a general human rights culture from which they feel alienated, perhaps because it challenges hierarchy within the Church. Thus life in Christ becomes a weak reflection of layered and graded society round about, and the salt loses its saltiness.

In view of equality's fundamental place in the Bible it is bad Christianity to treat people with any of the protected characteristics in English law as inferiors who fall short of a notional ideal. In the distant past this kind of treatment was thought appropriate for everyone from people with learning difficulties to the left-handed. Now it is as unacceptable – bad Christianity as well as an offence against what is often called, usually in scorn and ignorance, 'political correctness'.

Some people object that too much stress on equality makes everyone the same. Like uniqueness, equality cannot be qualified.

In fact, you cannot have too much or too little equality. Either people are equal or they are not. Neither is it possible to apply equality to identical objects. Equality is, in fact, the exact opposite of homogenisation. It acknowledges the differences between things, but offers them for comparison with one another using the test of interchangeability. This respects the God-given equal worth of each, whatever their functional differences, and reveals where justice lies between them.

It is hard to ignore the thought that there may be a correlation between homophobia and gender inequality. In Victorian times rigid legislation was passed against homosexual behaviour, but only for men. Like the Bible (with one exception in Romans 1), the discussion is entirely male.

The vast majority of voices raised in the public square about homosexuality are male. Why? To what extent is disgust about gayness related to fear of penetration? Certainly, the primitive condemnation in the book of Leviticus seems to be about men supposedly taking female subordinate sexual positions, whether voluntarily or as part of the humiliation of defeat in war.

Whatever we know about LGTBQI concerns, they are plainly far broader than simply one pattern of sexual behaviour. The exact number of gay people is unknown, and different surveys yield vastly different figures of between 2 per cent and 10 per cent who self-identify as gay. There is a higher degree of fluidity about sexuality among women than men. A far higher proportion of LGBTQI people are women than would be thought from many discussions of homosexuality. Allowing women to contribute more fully to the discussion might produce a more realistic and balanced debate, and shed new light on the subject.

Stephen Fry made a television series in 2013 travelling across the world to explore what it means to be gay.[11] He interviewed some of the world's most homophobic politicians and leaders in Uganda, the USA, Russia, Brazil and India. Sadly, certainly for those who believe faith has a positive role to play in the world, the prime motivation for these people's bigotry was religious. This makes it look as though faith and homophobia are inextricably linked. There are, of course, non-religious homophobes, but it may be they feel less entitled to articulate their anger openly.

Faith communities have their own particular forms of inertia in the face of change. They preserve and transmit traditional loyalties and dramatised frameworks for thought and reflection that would otherwise be lost for the future. They also have a valuable role in enriching public debate. Could they also have special opportunities to transform homophobic stuckness from within? To return to the basic question, 'Can gay people marry?', some Christians show self-awareness, humility, sensitivity to others, and often willingness to take change seriously. Perhaps faith can be part of the answer as well as the question. Much discussion and debate about this must centre, inevitably, on the Bible. How do we read it today? What does it actually say about gay people and marriage? Could it turn out to be a resource for positive change?

Scripture 101

For most faithful Christians, in various ways, the Bible is their ultimate authority. It is the source of God's truth to lighten their way and their map for the pilgrimage of faith.

Some people have suggested that the whole gay issue is actually really about the authority of the Bible. But before we can consider any texts in detail, we need to consider what the Bible is and how it is authoritative for faith. The Anglican Church does not have any mechanism for making dogma or even its own basis of faith. Since the sixteenth-century Reformation it has simply taken the historic creeds and Scriptures as normative, with no particular additions of its own.

How is the Bible authoritative? The traditional Anglican answer has been Article 6 of the 39 Articles, which dates back to 1549:

> Holy Scripture containeth all things necessary to salvation: so that whatsoever is not read therein, nor may be proved thereby, is not to be required of any man, that it should be believed an article of the Faith, or be thought requisite or necessary to salvation.

On the face of it, this is a very simple principle. Doing theology on this basis should be easy, but in practice is quite a trixical business. The logic is that of a restaurant that declares it is an eating house, and that meals will be served there whose ingredients will consist of food, but without saying which ones should be cooked on any particular day, or how.

As a result, down the years the words of Scripture, early tradition and sanctified reason have all played roles in the formation of faith. They have been blended variously by different people on different occasions for particular purposes. The principle laid down in Article 6 saves the bother of formulating the kind of Basis of Faith document many Evangelical organisations possess. It seldom manages to deliver pat answers to particular questions. This can be extremely frustrating for tidy-minded people.

Unlike the Holy Quran, or the Book of Mormon, the Bible can be translated into foreign languages. To a certain extent words' definitions are imported into the text by the reader from their own culture to determine the sense of the passage. Therefore the words themselves cannot be sacrosanct. This is as well because the texts that are being translated are not entirely certain. That is why very conservative biblicist statements of faith have to include a phrase like 'as originally given'. It acknowledges the gap between ideal and reality in the text, but makes a major unhistorical assumption about how the Bible was written.

Any human question can be answered, up to a point, by the dictionary. All the necessary words for a correct answer are in there somewhere. The clever bit, however, is digging out the best words in the right order. When it comes to reading the Bible every Christian community and individual has had their own way of doing this. The result is not quite total anarchy because common themes and meanings emerge from the text whenever it is read as authoritative.

The result of this is a paradox. Bible-believing Christians, taking the text neat, display the greatest confessional variety among themselves, reflected in the sheer number of Protestant denominations. The only way to find any common mind is to deem some matters more important than others. Some degree of dogmatic variation is inevitable. Orthodox Churches distil a wide body of patristic wisdom into norms and customs determined within each Patriarchate. The Roman Catholic Church has contained an amazing diversity. The magisterium has laid down dogma that is progressively more highly specified. The clearer and more dogmatic it has been, however, the more assiduously Catholic laity have found ways to ignore it. The practical result is greater variety, probably, than among Protestants and Orthodox Christians.

It follows that there are very few theological problems that can be solved definitively directly from the Bible. The way the Bible is being read needs to be carefully examined and reflected upon as it is read and applied.

Within the Judeo-Christian tradition prophetic texts only become authoritative as they are fulfilled:

> If a prophet speaks in the name of the LORD but the thing does not take place or prove true, it is a word that the LORD has not spoken. The prophet has spoken it presumptuously; do not be frightened by it.
>
> (Deuteronomy 18:22)

Prophetic words do not stand alone as absolute. They need to be made sure, confirmed by empirical fit. Their impact in real life needs to be assessed before their truth can be known. This is how Christian doctrine develops. The Bible text was generated and collected by the community from which it came, that defined it as authoritative. Handed down from generation to generation, that text has formed each new cohort of Christians according to unfolding and developing norms.

One might say, 'Christians should treat Bible texts the same way as Jesus did.' Unfortunately, that statement leaves various options open. Jesus knew and revered the Hebrew Scriptures, but also, on occasion, played fast and loose, radically extending conventional ways of applying what they were saying: 'You have heard that it was said "An eye for an eye and a tooth for a tooth"[Exodus 21:24] but I say to you, do not resist an evildoer'[Matthew 5:38–9].

Occasionally he applied verses directly to himself in surprising ways. Sometimes he laid aside what most took to be their plain meaning, for example by healing on the Sabbath.

Every Christian's starting point, however, has to be what the text actually says or doesn't say. This needs to be respected for what it is before being interpreted and applied. The culture from which it comes and to which it was originally addressed needs to be taken into account in reading it. This raises the question, 'If this is what it meant for them, what should it mean for us?'

Take one famous example, the story of Abraham offering to sacrifice his son Isaac (Genesis 22). The faith of Abraham is the foundational concept of Judaism, Christianity and Islam.

A crude fundamentalist reading would suggest a message that child sacrifice is a morally acceptable way for people to show how much they love God. When we examine the story in its historical context, however, other possible readings emerge. It came from the Canaanite Iron Age, when the sacrifice of firstborn children by fire in the wilderness was a perfectly normal thing to do. For people who believed this, this story actually establishes that child sacrifice is not necessary. God will provide what he wants, and that is a sacrificial lamb, not a child. Reading the text historically makes it applicable in future, way beyond its original time. This is part of what Christians mean when they see Scripture as living and active.

Interpretation is done on various levels. Take a non-historical story, Jesus' parable of the Pharisee and the publican (Luke 18:9–14). Both went up to the temple to pray, the former self-righteously while the latter sought God's mercy. How do we apply the story? One response might be, 'Let's thank God that we are not like the Pharisee.' The story itself, however, points towards a response that resonates on a deeper, meta, level. That way it illustrates the prophetic principle that God requires mercy not sacrifice. It also calls for a personal attitude like the publican's, not just imitation of the actions in the tale.

These basic principles about reading and applying the Bible are vital if the Scriptures are to be authoritative for Christians. Bandying around Bible soundbites trivialises Scripture and drains its meaning. The text needs to be taken very seriously and literally, but then interpreted in two worlds, the one from which it came and the one in which it is to be applied.

Literalism is never enough. The best way to call its bluff is to beat it at its own game. The city council of Shreveport, Louisiana, passed an ordinance banning housing or employment discrimination on the basis of sexual orientation or gender identity. It was opposed by Councilman Ron Webb, saying, 'The Bible tells you homosexuals are an abomination.' Ten days later, at an open meeting to consider repealing the measure, Pamela Raintree, a transgender woman, said:

> Leviticus 20:13 states, 'If a man also lie with mankind as he lieth with a woman, they shall surely put him to death.' I brought the first stone, Mr. Webb, in case that your Bible talk isn't just a smoke screen for personal prejudices.[1]

Webb withdrew his measure immediately, without calling for a vote.

Christians need to bear in mind what the Bible is, and how it informs faith today, as they ask twenty-first-century questions like 'Can gay people marry?' 'Is gay sex always wrong? and 'Are people married to transgender opposite-sex partners required, morally, to divorce?'

If we gathered the Bible writers around a conference table to answer these questions, they would need considerable explanation of the terminology. Biblical wisdom can be applied to the issues at stake, but not without translation. Godly logic derived from the Bible can engage with modern questions like 'How does paying taxes for socialised medicine modify any obligation to give alms?' or 'Is the development of nuclear power a good way to steward creation?' The process of finding the answer, however, is not simple or direct. It is silly, and flies in the face of the way Jesus and New Testament writers interpreted and applied their Scriptures contextually, to slap regulations designed for one age and place neatly on another.

It is impossible to scoop up Bible writers in a time machine and put them together. Therefore there is no alternative to using interpretative lenses to read the text. This will affect which verses we notice and select as significant, what we imagine they are saying, how we think they fit into the whole Bible story, and how we think they can be applied.

The first and most obvious fact about Scripture and homosexuality is that there is next to nothing there about it. Assuming that God gave us the Bible he wanted us to have, it is significant that only 0.002 per cent of Bible verses can possibly have anything to do with the subject directly. Compare and contrast the fact that some 10 per cent of Bible verses refer to matters of economic justice. This is an inconvenient truth for people who want to spin out whole books on the subject.

Given the wide range of sexual behaviour practised in the societies from which the Bible came, it is surprising that it should have so little to say about homosexuality. Bible writers generally show no shock-horror prurience about sex. Sexual behaviour is generally described actually and factually without varnish, prurience or titillation. Even the poetry of the Song of Songs is fairly down to earth. Scriptural awareness of sex is more Farmer Giles than E. L. James or Frankie Howerd.

We also have to remember with the question about gay people marrying that, as a matter of fact, the first English Bible to contain the word ' homosexual' was published in 1946. The origins of the word and concept itself are to be found around 1892. This makes it very unlikely that the Bible will yield a straightforward answer directly.

Sexual and social behaviour is understood vastly differently in different times and places, so we need to be very precise about definitions. We need to be equally precise about our own definitions and assumptions.

Conventionally minded people approach the text assuming that homosexuals are, in fact, heterosexuals, because everyone was created that way. What makes them gay is not nature, but a proclivity towards wrong behaviour. Its roots are an objective disorder, and it is also a sin against nature. If this complex of assumptions is made, every Bible verse that condemns immorality, adultery or licentiousness can then be applied, more or less, to homosexuals. This considerably swells the number of clobber texts available.

Other Bible readers, an increasing number in the West, define homosexuality as a phenomenon within, rather than against, nature. A Christian with this definition would see it as an aspect of the way God made the world. People who do not see being LGBTQI as a sin, or an illness in itself, will then apply the same moral standard for behaviour to all equally. Jesus applied the term 'adulterous' to a whole generation. This does not mean he believed every one of them was indulging in penetrative sex with someone else's spouse. The adultery Jesus condemned was a general attitude of sexual unfaithfulness that could apply to same-sex couples in much the same way as anyone else.

These ways of reading the text, hostile or friendly to LGBTQI people, affect which verses are selected as relevant, what the reader thinks they are saying when they read them, the composite picture of the whole Bible narrative into which they are fitted, and the preferences people will have in applying them.

How is it best to read the text?

First, readers need to respect the integrity of the whole text, within the historical context from which it came. There may be various ways to interpret the text, but not until we have established what it says in the first place. This means assuming that things mean what they say, however welcome, unwelcome or unusual they may seem. Confronted, for example, with a text that suggests that small boys who mock a prophet's baldness should be torn to bits by bears (2 Kings 2:23–24), we must not pretend it is saying more or less than it is. Acknowledging the actuality of the text does not require us to murder small boys who laugh at teachers, but it does draw attention to a very different aspect of the culture from which it came. Our reaction to it helps to log and understand where we are now, different as it has to be.

We must also respect the integrity of the whole text of which every verse forms a part. So, for example, when we read an ancient law code within the book of Leviticus, it is questionable to chop the text into tiny pieces and assign entirely different significance to each in relation to its neighbours. Every commandment is a commandment, and was intended to be so.

The text invites us to read every verse, as well as all the verses together. The more obscure ones need to be questioned harder, but not discarded. For example, it may seem very odd that the Law of Moses (Exodus 23:19, 24–26 and Deuteronomy 14:21) forbids people from seething a kid in its mother's milk. The rabbis went on to ask many questions about why this should be so, but they did not, out of reverence, simply shrug the text aside, as Christian readers are prone to do.

Secondly, bits of the Bible, after being read in their own terms historically and within their close context, have to be placed within the whole Bible. Thus a Bible macro narrative emerges from its micro narratives.

Photo mosaics assemble multitudes of tiny pictures in a way that, zoomed out, become a single large image. Each picture has its own integrity, but only by standing back and examining the whole can we understand the true potential locked up in single verses and stories.

Thus the story of the Exodus resonates throughout the Hebrew Scriptures and is picked up by New Testament writers in many different ways. It comes to life, again and again, as a grand narrative of liberation when it is applied to the historical circumstances of, for example, slaves in the nineteenth-century USA or the poor in contemporary Latin America.

The Evangelical theologian Mark Noll has researched how the American Civil War could be called a theological as well as a political crisis.[2] It appears that nineteenth-century US Christians, almost all of them professed Bible believers, understood Bible teaching about the morality of slavery in very different ways.

Two incompatible grand narratives emerged.

The first took the many Bible texts that legitimate, endorse or regulate slavery literally and interpreted them prescriptively to justify what was going on in the plantations. They accused abolitionists of ignoring and subverting the Bible text.

The second started with a conviction that the golden rule applied to blacks in the same way as to anyone else. British Quakers and Evangelicals had staked out new moral high ground in the eighteenth century with newly perceived equality that saw the black man as a man and a brother. This broad-gauge reading de-emphasised pro-slavery Bible passages and highlighted what Martin Luther King was to call the broad arc of the Bible story. Thus Scripture was read as a freedom song that justified, indeed required, abolition.

People who supported both broad-gauge and narrow-gauge narratives knew and used the Bible intensively to advance their causes and were, naturally, entirely correct in their own terms.

Christian attitudes to other moral issues reproduced the same patterns of Bible interpretation.

Up to the mid-twentieth century child-beating was seen as morally improving, or at least necessary. The Bible clearly mandated it. British teaching unions campaigned, as late as the 1980s, for their members to be allowed to beat schoolchildren. When the practice was abolished, some conservative Christian groups pursued a campaign in the courts to preserve it in their schools as biblical discipline.[3]

Similarly Anglican bishops worked energetically until well into the twentieth century to preserve capital punishment, on biblical grounds.[4] At the same time others, motivated as they saw it by Christian love and the requirements of true justice, worked for abolition of hanging on the basis of their broad-gauge reading of the Bible.

We, who approach Bible texts with modern questions, need to be careful, mindful of our own assumptions and proclivities and especially aware about the relationship between the things that can be read out of the text and the things we have already read into it. This substantial health warning applies supremely to the classical 'clobber texts' that have been applied to gay people. These need to be examined before we can move on to the question of whether or not gay people can be allowed to marry.

Things gays are liable to read in the Bible

There are 31,240 verses in the Christian Bible.

Five passages refer directly to behaviour that could have anything to do with what we call homosexuality:

- *Genesis 19* – God's judgement of Sodom

- *Leviticus 18:22 and 20:13* – A priestly holiness code

- *Romans 1:26–7* – Gentiles are liable for their idolatry

- *1 Corinthians 6:9* – A list of kingdom-denying vices

- *1 Timothy 1:10* – Wrongdoers subject to legal sanction.

Any biblical argument that homosexuality is either non-existent or intrinsically morally disordered is based on a tiny handful of words and sound bites. These so-called 'clobber texts' are few and far between but have been massively influential in the Church's dealings with LGBTQI people.

Genesis 19

The story of Sodom is to be found in Genesis, the first book of the Bible. What went on there was utterly depraved. A group of young men in the city attempted a frenzy of group sex with two visiting male strangers. This sin made God so angry that he destroyed the whole place with fire and brimstone, along with its twin city, Gomorrah, where the same kind of debauchery was doubtless going on. These cities of the plain became a byword for wickedness. The story is crudely used to demonstrate that God disapproves of gay sex.

To understand what the story actually says, we need to read it in its context, the age of the patriarchs.

In Genesis 13, Abram, known later as Abraham, and his nephew Lot go their separate ways. Lot settles near Sodom, whose inhabitants are said to be very wicked, greatly sinning against the Lord. We are not, at this stage, told exactly how.

Next up in the narrative come a series of blessings on Abram and his house, culminating in a significant close encounter between the newly rebranded Abraham and three angels near the Oaks of Mamre.

This story is familiar to millions of Christians, pictured in a famous twelfth-century Russian icon of the Holy Trinity to be found in many Churches and most retreat centres. It shows Abraham entertaining the mysterious three, prefiguring the hospitality of God inviting us to share in the love that unites Father, Son and Holy Spirit. On the table lies a sacrifice. The angels are shown as guests around the table, bearing symbols of authority. Viewers of the Rublev icon who like to think the eyes of portraits in stately homes follow them round the room will see themselves as the fourth guest, completing the circle.

Lot's journey into the Jordan rift valley following the parting of the ways in chapter 13 was altogether less auspicious.

After an adventure that saw Lot a prisoner of war needing to be rescued by his uncle Abram, he settles back in Sodom. In Genesis 19, two of the angels who had been received graciously in Mamre arrive in the city, disguised in human form.

Lot invites them into his home, as is his duty. Just as Uncle Abraham had done, he prepares them a meal. But soon there is shouting in the street outside and a group of men from Sodom bang on the door. They demand that Lot bring out his guests so that they can have sex with them. Lot refuses to do this, but offers them his two virgin daughters instead as substitutes.

But guests, he says, should not be raped, 'for they have come under the protection of my roof'. This argument fails to impress the gang of yobs. They try to break down the door, but the angels strike them with blindness. They warn Lot to flee the city because 'the outcry to the LORD against its people is so great that he has sent us to destroy it.'

Retribution follows swiftly. God destroys both cities of the plain, Sodom and Gomorrah, with fire and brimstone. Their very names become a byword and a curse. Isaiah uses them, shockingly, to describe Judah as a sinful nation. Jeremiah 23:14 says that sinners who commit adultery, idolatry, and false prophecy make themselves like the people of Sodom. Amos 4:11 calls those who proudly oppress the poor and crush the needy 'people of Sodom'. Zephaniah 2:9 foresees the same judgement on foreigners who taunt God's people.

What exactly was the sin of Sodom? It has to have been broader than simply the incident recounted against Lot's guests, for God had said that if he could even find ten righteous in the city he would spare it. The clearest description of the sin of Sodom in the Hebrew Scriptures occurs in the prophecy of Ezekiel 16:48–50

> This was the guilt of your sister Sodom: she and her daughters had pride, excess of food, and prosperous ease, but did not aid the poor and needy. They were haughty, and did abominable things before me; therefore I removed them when I saw it.

Among the characters in Genesis 19, only the angels come out particularly well. Lot offered his visitors hospitality, but he was less than the ideal father, offering his virgin daughters to the mob instead. We are told in 2 Peter 2:7–10 that God rescued Lot, 'a righteous man greatly distressed by the licentiousness of the lawless (for that righteous man, living among them day after day, was tormented in his righteous soul by their lawless deeds that he saw and heard)'.

The moral drawn from the tale here is that 'the LORD knows how to rescue the godly from trial, and to keep the unrighteous under punishment until the day of judgement'.

The prime sin of Sodom arose from the intent of the rapists. This was a gang rape, not an orgy, which indicated a generally sinful way of life within the city. Its essence was moral recklessness and violence, rather than its sexual orientation. The gang rape of female strangers would have been as bad.

Judges 19 tells the story of an old man being treated similarly to the angels in Sodom by the inhabitants of Gibeah. This mob also refuses the host's offer of his virgin daughter as a substitute, on the grounds that she is not a guest. But on this occasion, the host brings out his concubine to the rapists, who abuse her all night. Having been raped, the hapless girl is dismembered by her owner, who sends the pieces of her body around the tribes of Israel, to summon a posse to avenge her.

These gang rapes, real or intended, were a particularly heinous crime in a society with a strong code of hospitality to strangers.

The same-sex dimension of the sin of Sodom must not be allowed to dominate. It is worth noting in Judges 19 that when a domestic concubine is substituted for a visiting stranger, 'the worst thing that has been seen or done since the day the Israelites came up out of Egypt' happens. God does not, however, punish the whole city by destroying it, as he did Sodom. The sin of Sodom was a broad spectrum criminality that went down in history as archetypal rebellion against righteousness. Only homophobic interpretations will see any need to narrow it into an objection to homosexuality in itself. There is no evidence in the text that God would have spared the city if the yobs had taken Lot up on the offer of his daughters.

The memory of the cities of the plain and their fate became a dreadful warning. In the gospels, Jesus sends out his disciples with the admonishment that any village that does not welcome these strangers as messengers of the Lord (like the angels in the story of Abram and Lot) will suffer a worse fate on the day of judgement than Sodom and Gomorrah. The Sodomites' inhospitality contrasts painfully with the way the angels had been received by Abram at Mamre.

The sin of Sodom was even worse, one New Testament writer suggests, because the strangers happened to be angels. A strange verse in Jude 7 says that the rapists, in the quaint words of the King James Bible, were 'giving themselves over to fornication, and going after strange flesh'.

The flesh lusted after in Genesis 19 was not that of men, but angels. Therefore, close reading of the letter shows its principal target is actually those who mess with spiritual powers, or gang rape angels (if not just strangers), a sin of which few can be accused these days, gay or straight.

This behaviour violates the important principle of difference in the Hebrew law: 'You shall not let your animals breed with a different kind; you shall not sow your field with two kinds of seed; nor shall you put on a garment made of two different materials' (Leviticus 19:19). However much we sexualise the Epistle of Jude's strange phrase it cannot thus refer to homosexuality, which in no way violates the law's principle of sameness.

From the time of Jesus on, swelling to a mighty flood in the Middle Ages, readers of Genesis 19 narrowed their focus, increasingly obsessionally, onto the orientation of the intended rape. The sin of Sodom became simply sex between men. Written for Pope Leo IX around 1049, eleventh-century Peter Damian's *Book of Gomorrah* proposed refusing ordination to such 'Sodomites', and left its readers in no doubt about the sin, or its consequences:

> The miserable flesh burns with the heat of lust; the cold mind trembles with the rancour of suspicion; and in the heart of the miserable man chaos boils like Tartarus ... In fact, after this most poisonous serpent once sinks its fangs

into the unhappy soul, sense is snatched away, memory is borne off, the sharpness of the mind is obscured. It becomes unmindful of God and even forgetful of itself. This plague undermines the foundation of faith, weakens the strength of hope, destroys the bond of charity; it takes away justice, subverts fortitude, banishes temperance, blunts the keenness of prudence. And what more should I say since it expels the whole host of the virtues from the chamber of the human heart and introduces every barbarous vice as if the bolts of the doors were pulled out.[1]

By the eve of the fourteenth century Peter Damien's sort of disgust gave birth to a new term that entered the English language in 1297, 'the vyle sunne of sodomye'.[2]

These crude medieval tirades, which have nothing to do with the real meaning of the texts on which they were based, sound quaint to modern ears but, alarmingly, their echoes can still be heard in the Church today.

Leviticus 18:22 and 20:13

The book of Leviticus contains what is apparently the clearest and most obvious condemnation of homosexuality in the Bible. Two verses from it are often quoted to settle the matter at one fell swoop.

Leviticus 18:22 says that it is detestable for a man to lie with another man, as with a woman. A later verse (20:13) says the same thing, but adds that in these circumstances both should be put to death, with their blood upon their own heads.

The word for a detestable act, colourfully translated by the King James Bible as 'abomination', is most accurately translated as a 'abhorrence' or 'taboo' – exceptional behaviour characteristic of foreigners that blurs the line between the people of Israel and the rest of the world. Thus it is used for child sacrifice, witchcraft and intermarriage with foreigners

(Malachi 2:11), cross dressing (Deureronomy 22:5), marrying a divorced woman (Deuteronomy 24:4), sacrificing blemished animals (Deuteronomy 17:1), and even (for Egyptians) eating with foreigners (Genesis 43:32 and 46:34).[3]

What exactly do these verses condemn? Literally, 'a male lying with a male, the lyings (or beds) of a woman'. Most Hebrew descriptions of sexual activity, involve euphemism, but this seems pretty graphic. The essence of the offence seems to be a man taking a female sexual position in bed with another man. This echoes depictions of male-on-male rape as an act of war or cultic prostitution in the ancient near East.

> The rape of a defeated male enemy was considered the special right of the victorious soldier in some societies and was a signal of the totality of the defeat. There was a widespread belief that a male who was sexually penetrated, even if it was by forced sexual assault, thus 'lost his manhood,' and could no longer be a warrior or ruler.[4]

This taboo is also about gender. In a society which viewed women as inferior, for a man to submit to the kind of treatment a woman would receive in bed was shameful. In his *Life of Abraham*, the first-century AD commentator Philo says the problem was men being treated like women and thus becoming addicted to effeminacy and delicacy and corrupting their souls.[5]

To be precise, the Leviticus prohibitions seem to refer to penetrative sex between two men, where one plays what was understood at the time to be a female role. It says nothing about any form of same-sex activity between women.

How, then, could a married gay couple understand and apply this law to their lives? There is, actually, no requirement for spouses to engage in any particular sexual activity in order to be married. Those who engage in heterosexual marriage are not required to take any particular position in bed. Therefore, it would be inaccurate to make this text a simple prohibition of gay people marrying. A gay married couple might decide on its basis that they were going to abstain from anal sex with a male taking what in the world of Leviticus would be thought a female position. As we have seen, the vast majority of gay couples do not, research suggests, engage in anal sex anyway.[6]

There are various ways to describe this prohibition in its close context. The regulations of Leviticus encompass a wide variety of behaviours.

The verses that forbid males bedding other males as women occur amid prohibitions of incest, bestiality and the sacrifice of children. We would hold all these to be morally wrong, not just foreign practices.

A reader who found Leviticus obsolete might point out that the code to which this prohibition belongs also proscribes deceased wife's sister marriages and sleeping with menstruating women, along with crossbreeding animals, planting a field with two kinds of seed, fiddling weights or wages, wearing mixed fibre clothing, or picking fruit from a tree during its first three years. What we have here is a morally mixed bag, each element of which needs to be assessed today on its own merits.

How can modern Christians relate to the Leviticus holiness code? It explains some details of Old Testament moral logic. None of the practices it condemns are merely ceremonial or connected particularly with the sacrificial system. The whole book includes food laws which Jewish people still apply literally, from which most Christians regard themselves as free. Christians can read the book as illustrative material, weighing each individual proscription in its own terms.

Different Christians will decide which to take upon themselves and how, discerning the matter within the Christian community, bearing in mind St Paul's principle that each one should be convinced in their own mind. They also need to consider his other principle that those who follow slavishly the basic requirement of the law about circumcision are actually binding themselves to the lot (Galatians 5:2–4).

As well as considering what the Old Testament forbids in the bedroom, we might note in passing what it requires. Levirate marriage (Deuteronomy 25:5–10) requires a man to marry his brother's widow to produce an heir. Both polygamy and concubinage are pretty much assumed in the Hebrew Scriptures; indeed, it is arguable that the vast majority of marriages in the Bible would not pass muster as marriages in the modern West.

Romans 1:26–27

The New Testament contains one clear and significant text that, in itself, has often been used as a simple knockdown condemnation of all homosexual orientation and activity. This passage is also significant as the only one which refers to same-sex attraction between women. This may matter especially to the substantial number of gay and bisexual people who are women.

St Paul, as he opens his letter to the Romans can be understood to condemn every form of same-sex attraction outright. He is laying out his great themes about God and judgement, and begins by establishing the moral responsibility of Gentiles to the God of the Hebrews. He turns to the mystery of Jewish sin and rejection of God soon enough, but for now we can easily imagine Jewish Christians cheering him along as he demolishes any attempt Gentiles might make to wriggle out of their moral responsibility to God.

From the beginning the Creator of heaven and earth has revealed his power and divine nature through creation. Therefore no one can have any excuse. Yet degraded pagans have swapped the worship of God for that of his creatures:

> For this reason God gave them up to degrading passions. Their women exchanged natural intercourse for unnatural, and in the same way also the men, giving up natural intercourse with women, were consumed with passion for one another. Men committed shameless acts

with men and received in their own persons the due penalty for their error.

Plainly, St Paul does not approve of people exchanging what he sees as their natural orientation for same-sex attraction, any more than he condones the bigger sin of which he sees it to be a part, idolatry that worships the creation not the creator.

In this context, St Paul applies the term 'unnatural' to same-sex attraction. That word has long played a powerful role in anti-gay rhetoric. Many conventionally brought-up people would say same-sex attraction flies in the face of nature. But what does St Paul mean by 'nature'?

St Paul's world takes in two different concepts, 'nature' and 'creation'. Creation is the order God has established from the beginning. It groans in travail, awaiting its liberation, the redemption of the body.

The term 'nature', however, denotes human convention, custom or expectation. Therefore in 1 Corinthians 11:14 St Paul asks his readers, 'Does not nature itself teach you that if a man wears long hair, it is degrading to him?' With a twenty-first-century understanding of sexual orientation and gender, it would be rather adventurous, foolish even, to suppose these verses constitute a grand theory to explain same-sex attraction. There is considerably more to the matter. At most, Romans 1 can only refer directly to people we would call 'bisexual'. It says nothing about gay people who have never felt a shred of attraction to the opposite sex, sometimes having sought it with many tears and even reparative 'therapy'.

To understand Romans 1, we have to read verses 25–27 carefully in the context of the larger argument of which it is a small part. St Paul is setting out his stall here, stripping away any claim pagans might have that God's judgement does not apply to them. In this passage same-sex attraction is the punishment, not the crime.

The crime is idolatry – substituting creation for the Creator – by worshipping 'images resembling a mortal human being, or birds, or four-footed animals or reptiles'.

This sin is evidence of deep alienation from God, for which Gentiles are morally and spiritually accountable, as much as Jews who are expected to keep their more explicit divine law. Ancient cities were crowded with shrines where there was an unmissable connection between idolatry and all kinds of sexual behaviour.

What does this incidental observation by St Paul mean for a faithful couple of gay Christians in the twenty-first century? It is hard to see how these words can be thought to apply in any simple way to people who, without any idolatrous attitude or belief, have not done the action that is condemned. It is addressed to Gentiles and means that all have sinned and fallen short of God's glory, with or without the Hebrew Scriptures to guide them.

1 Corinthians 6:9 and 1 Timothy 1:10

What remains as biblical evidence against homosexuality are two lists of vices.

The 1 Corinthians list includes a Greek term that literally means 'softies'(*malakoi*).[7] It is used of clothes as well as people. Some commentators sexualise its meaning into a technical term for 'gay males who allow themselves to be penetrated', although there is another perfectly good Greek word that carries a more narrowly sexualised meaning. The term St Paul uses here, in fact, crops up all over ancient literature and can mean 'effeminate' but includes a wide range of self-indulgent behaviours, including liking soft clothing, warm baths, gourmet food, decadence, or cowardice. Considering the term alongside the others in the vice list of which it forms a part, a very broad swathe of bad behaviour is said here to be incompatible with inheriting the kingdom of God – idolatry, adultery, theft, drunkenness, slander, greed, fraud. Some gay males may be 'softies' but there are plenty of heterosexual 'softies' out there.

Another more significant term occurs in both vice lists. This literally means, 'male-bedders' (*arsenokoites*).[8] St Paul coined the term himself. Its precise meaning, as originally written, cannot be authenticated from previous authors. It seems probable that St Paul, steeped in the Hebrew Scriptures, could well have quarried the raw materials for his word from a place where its two components occur close together – the Greek translation of the book of Leviticus, and the verses we have already considered in chapters 18 and 21.

If this is the case, what he would have had in mind is the sin of a passive male partner who allows himself to be bedded as though he were a woman. The 'male-bedder' in New Testament vice lists, however, is treated as though his sin involves more than simply being in bed with another man. Often this misdemeanour figures among economic rather than narrowly sexual sins. Sexual behaviour is involved, but in the context of profiteering or exploiting others. Perhaps we are talking about something more like 'rent boys' pimps' than consenting adult partners.

In both New Testament passages St Paul's new word 'male-bedder' occurs after sexually motivated sins like licentiousness, adultery and lewdness, and up against economic and social crimes – theft, greed and fraud (1 Corinthians) and slave trafficking, lying and perjury (1 Timothy). This context makes it look as though what is being condemned is some kind of sexual exploitation.

In later literature St Paul's new word occurs very occasionally but almost never as a narrowly sexual sin. The second-century Sibylline Oracles, for example, place it squarely within the category of social and economic wrongdoing:

> do not steal seed.
> Accursed through many generations he
> who took it unto scattering of life.

Indulge not vile lusts ['male-bed'] slander not, nor kill.
Give too-worn his hire; Do not afflict
the poor man.[9]

In the same sort of way, another second-century writing, *The Acts of John,* warns: 'Let the murderer know that the merited punishment is double in the time after he goes from here! In like manner, the poisoner, sorcerer, robber, defrauder, sodomite [male-bedder], thief, and all who belong to that band ...'[10]

Precise definitions elude us again, but, as we found in Romans 1, there is no need to take these vice lists as a blanket condemnation of all same-sex attraction. Something more specific seems to be in mind.

It is an argument from silence, but had any late Hellenistic writer wished to condemn consenting adult male lovers there were various perfectly common words with which to do this. The most credible option is to view the new term 'male-bedder' as referring to men who practise abusive or exploitative sex, perhaps some form of trafficking. This could be particularly prevalent in pagan temples with their plentiful rent boys.

In summary, the tiny collection of New Testament texts that make any reference to same-sex activity can be understood in many different ways. Translators and commentators in every age are understandably radicalised when they encounter a subject about which they are particularly sensitised in a Scripture. In much the same way as good Catholics tend to see visions of the Virgin Mary while Buddhists see visions of the Buddha, people who are for or against homosexuality develop self-consistent readings that are either pro- or anti-gay, and all stops in between.

What of the broad-gauge narrative? Many will interpret the detailed text within the broader teaching of the Sermon on the Mount. This calls into question all legalism and prefigures the radical principle laid down by St Paul in Romans 13:8–9:

> Owe no one anything, except to love one another; for the one who loves another has fulfilled the law. The commandments, 'You shall not commit adultery; You shall not murder; You shall not steal; You shall not covet'; and any other commandment, are summed up in this word, 'Love your neighbour as yourself.' Love does no wrong to a neighbour; therefore, love is the fulfilling of the law.

It is easy, but not necessary, to break these texts down into their components in order to extract technical terminology that can then be broadened out and laid on LGBTQI people as condemnation.

In fact, approaches to ancient texts that rely too heavily on analysing vocabulary can easily mislead. For example, we may note that the origins of the English word 'holiday' are to be found in two basic words, 'holy' and 'day'. True as this fact is, it will shed no light on the word's actual meaning. If someone tells you they are going on holiday, this is not a way of saying they are really going on a pilgrimage. If they were they would probably use the obvious other word.

Therefore gay-friendly readers are bound to notice the complete absence in the New Testament of any of the extensive standard assortment of Greek words that would have been used naturally to describe the enormous amount of same-sex activity that went on in ancient cities.

Christians understand the Scriptures as part of the Good News of Jesus Christ:

> You will know them by their fruits. Are grapes gathered from thorns, or figs from thistles? In the same way, every good tree bears good fruit, but the bad tree bears bad fruit. A good tree cannot bear bad fruit, nor can a bad tree bear good fruit …

> (Matthew 7:16–18)

The Scriptures cannot bear bitter fruit. The discipline that enables Christians to hear the word of God according to the love of God is not woolly liberalism, but obedience to the New Testament injunction to discern the spirits and make love our aim.

Biblical marriage

Those searching the Scriptures with the twenty-first-century question 'Can gay people marry?' will approach the text with very different cultural baggage.

All of us over a certain age were brought up in a profoundly homophobic society. For the first 12 years of my life gay sex was illegal. Social attitudes softened in the years that followed. Another few years, and the idea that gayness was some kind of mental illness passed away. There was a certain amount of music hall ribaldry around it, but people became increasingly less nasty about gay people. Homophobia's final frontier, however, is its fundamental assumption that the sexualities of LGBTQI people are somehow anomalous, whether culpably, as people thought in the 1950s, or clinically, as was believed in the 1970s.

My personal context coloured the way in which I first read the Bible. I always wanted to be nice about it, but, even more than science, it was getting to know real gay people that changed my mind. The present generation of young people live in a society which still suffers from more ingrained prejudice than most of us would care to admit. They do not, however, suffer from the profound structural homophobia of the culture in which I grew up, which shaped the definitions of the words I thought I was reading in the Bible.

What can a reader who does not see homosexuality as deviance make of the Bible? What does it say about marriage anyway, and the possibility that gay people might be able to marry?

No Bible writer would recognise terms like homosexual and heterosexual, any more than they would other modern words like 'paranoia', 'inflation' or 'electricity'. This does not mean that people in Bible times could not be mentally unbalanced, or that the value of their money was constant, or the fundamental physics of the universe was different. All these things, however, were understood very differently. Therefore careful translation is necessary, as always, if we are to apply biblical wisdom to our lives in a way that is good news.

As we turn to what the Bible says about marriage, it is sometimes suggested that from time immemorial: 'I conceive that marriage, as understood in Christendom, may for this purpose be defined as the voluntary union for life of one man and one woman, to the exclusion of all others.'[1]

This definition, minus mention of Christendom, used to hang on the walls of register offices. Registrars used to quote it during marriage ceremonies, with the preface 'marriage, according to the law of this country is …'.

At first hearing, this definition sounds timeless and absolute. In fact, this definition of marriage comes not from the Bible but a Victorian judge, Lord Penzance. The Purpose of which he spoke was assessing the legal status of Mormonism and polygamy in the leading case of *Hyde v. Hyde and Woodmansee* (1866).

His words exude Victorian clarity and self-confidence. Surely, people might think, since the time of Adam and Eve, voluntary monogamy of a man and a woman for life was always the norm. Unfortunately, however, very few marriages in the Bible involved anything of the sort.

The Hebrew Scriptures contain at least seven different definitions of marriage. Adam and Eve sound like the original simple nuclear family, one plus one for life. In a way, that was all they could be, since they were the only two people in the world at the time. Generally speaking, Old Testament marriage customs and mores reflect the social mores of the people in the story.

In Genesis 38, Levirate marriage comes on the scene. This is the involuntary marriage of a man to his brother's widow in order to continue the line. This kind of marriage was still theoretically current enough in Jesus' day for it to be the basis of a question the Sadducees asked him about a bride, seven brothers and resurrection (Matthew 22:23–32). In 1509, this was the basis on which Henry VIII believed his marriage to Catherine of Aragon was legitimate, but by mid-1526 he had decided otherwise. Meanwhile Catherine maintained that her earlier marriage to Henry's brother Arthur had never been consummated.

Deuteronomy 22:28–29 institutes another involuntary form of marriage. A virgin automatically becomes the wife of her rapist, who is then required to pay the victim's father 50 shekels for the loss of his property rights. Unlike other Old Testament marriages, these are held to be indissoluble.

In Numbers 31:17–18 we find another form of involuntary marriage. A male soldier is entitled to take as many virgins as he likes for his wives from among his booty, but must kill his other prisoners.

In Deuteronomy 21:11–14, marriage is made by selecting a beautiful woman from among the spoils of war, shaving her head and paring her nails. These marriages are dissoluble if she fails to please, but the woman is no longer saleable.

Throughout much of the Old Testament, marriage does not require sexual exclusivity. Concubines are allowed, alongside wives. Abraham had only two concubines, where Solomon had 300, along with his 700 wives (1 Kings 11:3).

The basic principle of these relationships is that if a woman's father pays a man to take her away, she's his wife. If he pays her father to take her away, she's his concubine. This is many light years away from the prim Victorian world of Lord Penzance, let alone *Brides* magazine. As was generally the case in pre-modern societies, biblical marriages were basically dynastic arrangements, and most seem to have been polygamous.

They were also, very much, property transactions. This can be seen clearly in the narrative of King David's adultery with Bathsheba (2 Samuel 11:1–12:12). The king sees a beautiful woman bathing on the roof, then arranges for her husband, Uriah the Hittite, to be placed in the front line. Soon afterwards he is killed. His death allows David, morally speaking, to steal her for his own. Technically, David has broken no rules. Sexual desire is involved, but the prophet Nathan does not confront King David on these grounds. Rather, he tells the story of a rich man who steals sheep from a poor neighbour. Once David's indignation is aroused against the thief, Nathan calls him out by announcing that David is the thief. His crime is a property matter.

Compared to Lord Penzance's definition, almost all Old Testament marriages are involuntary for at least one of the parties, usually the wife. They are not for life, but dissolvable at will by the man, if not the woman. Far from excluding all others, they often include surprising other parties.

Above all, a wife is defined as her husband's property. The point is forcefully made to those who attend Holy Communion services according to the Book of Common Prayer, with the Ten Commandments recited in full. Here, the celebrant tells the men in the congregation: 'Thou shalt not covet thy neighbour's wife. Thou shall not covet thy neighbour's maid, nor his ox, nor his ass, nor any other Thing that is his.'

At the time of Lord Penzance's judgement, English women were still their husband's property, subject to the ancient doctrine of couverture. This aspect of wedlock, dating back to time immemorial, was done away with in England 15 years later when marriage was fundamentally redefined by the Married Women's Property Act (1881).

What about marriage in the New Testament?

Jesus gladly participated in a wedding feast at Cana of Galilee. He first revealed his glory to his disciples by relieving the family's embarrassment when it ran out of wine. One of the stranger letters I have received since coming out as a supporter of gay people being able to marry was from a woman whose argument was to assert that had the wedding in Cana of Galilee been a same-sex marriage, the Jesus in whom she believed would not have bothered to turn up. There is no way of proving this notion to be wrong, but it probably tells us more about her than about Jesus.

We do know, however, that Jesus emphatically refused to involve himself in family inheritance disputes (Luke 12:13–14). He taught that marriage was, technically, a secular matter. This is not 'secular' in the modern sense of being generally anti-God, but 'secular' in the sense of 'belonging to this passing age'. In the world to come, Jesus taught, no one will be married or given in marriage (Matthew 22:30). The age of the Messiah will see perfect equality between God's children, with no one owning others, through slavery or marriage. Family ties, immensely strong in the society to which Jesus spoke, will be irrelevant at kingdom come.

If marriage is firmly part of the temporal order and not eternal, it seems logical that many aspects of marriage will be impermanent, liable to change with every particular passing age. This is exactly how things have unfolded. Much to the anger and frustration of those who may want to see Jesus as the originator of the modern nuclear family, he never married. He distanced himself from his own family in a way that would have seemed shocking at the time. Told that his family are outside waiting to see him, Jesus replied:

> 'Who is my mother, and who are my brothers?' And pointing to his disciples, he said, 'Here are my mother and my brothers! For whoever does the will of my Father in heaven is my brother and sister and mother.'
>
> (Matthew 12:48–50)

This aspect of Jesus' teaching was strongly countercultural at the time. There was within Judaism as he knew it a strong

presumption that everyone would marry. Jesus emphatically does
not share it, and questions, radically, the social structure of the
family. Clan loyalty, however powerful in first-century Palestine,
comes second to discipleship in the kingdom of a Master who
came to bring a sword not peace. Walking authentically in its
ways will sometimes bring persecution, Jesus taught, in language
echoing the prophet Micah (7:6):

> For I have come to set a man against his Father,
> and a daughter against her mother,
> and a daughter-in-law against her mother-in-law;
> and one's foes will be members of one's own
> household.

> Whoever loves father or mother more than me is not
> worthy of me; whoever loves son or daughter more than
> me is not worthy of me; and whoever does not take up
> the cross and follow me is not worthy of me. Those who
> find their life will lose it, and those who lose their life for
> my sake will find it.

> (Matthew 10:35–39)

If this teaching means anything, any organisation seriously
trying to follow Jesus will be careful and wary about investing
too much of itself in the institutions of marriage and family.
Both are transient and belong to the present passing age not the
world to come. Jesus' followers should not be surprised to find
that as the ages unfold marriage changes all the time.

Jesus and his disciples treated marriage and family with the same
practical but not absolute respect as the other social institutions
of their day, slavery, race and gender. All are provisional and
subservient to the kingdom. St Paul further puts matters more
positively in the famous verse where he declares: 'There is no
longer Jew or Greek, there is no longer slave or free, there is no

longer male and female; for all of you are one in Christ Jesus' (Galatians 3:28).

Engaging with the great sources of hierarchy and belonging in the ancient world, he proclaims Christ transcends them. It is hard to square the passage with any form of hard subordination, within or outside marriage, especially when it is based on race, gender or slavery.

Jesus teaches that marriage is a provisional institution with roots in creation. Like the Sabbath, it was created for people not people for the Sabbath. It is a way of arranging other matters of this age, like property, inheritance and dynastic legitimacy, all of them less important than the kingdom. Its deepest meaning, however, arises from the way people were created.

Jesus stays well out of family disputes, but criticises the scribes and Pharisees for allowing the systems and processes regulating divorce to obliterate the original point of marriage. Thus he locates marriage away from the realm of law that the scribes inhabit and control, and roots it in the story of Adam and Eve. Those who believe in the Janet and John binary theory of sex and gender will see his reference to Genesis as importing gender into his definition of marriage. We may notice, however, something that later Christians were sometimes to notice, that before the Fall the prime purpose of Eve was friendship not sex. Many of his contemporaries would have said a man who failed to marry was defying his creation purpose. Not Jesus. Permanent, faithful, stable marriage is not for everyone. Reacting to its absolute demands, 'His disciples said to him, "If such is the case of a man with his wife, it is better not to marry." But he said to them, "Not everyone can accept this teaching, but only those to whom it is given"' (Matthew 19:10–11).

Human capacity bears on the matter. Nor does Jesus see the way people are made for marriage, or not in simple binary terms. His teaching on divorce in Matthew's gospel ends with some fascinating but obscure verses. This uses the terminology of the day, but violates radically the prohibition in Deuteronomy 23:1

of eunuchs in the house of God. Echoing Isaiah 53:3–5, Jesus promises a broad range of possibilities for the unmarriageable as those acceptable to God:

> For there are eunuchs who have been so from birth, and there are eunuchs who have been made eunuchs by others, and there are eunuchs who have made themselves eunuchs for the sake of the kingdom of heaven. Let anyone accept this who can.
>
> (Matthew 19:12)

The institution of marriage is made for people, not people for the institution. Human capacity drives right practice. Jesus relates the social obligation to marry to the different ways different people seem to be made.

One size emphatically does not fit all. He recognises four different sorts of people in the world, only the first the natural marrying kind. Others do not marry because of the way they are from birth, or because other people forbid their marriages, or because they have embraced celibacy for the kingdom. Shockingly for his age, his words provide a charter for celibacy as much as for marriage.

Those who believe homosexuality is an objective disorder may miss the significance of these verses as a charter for celibacy as much as marriage, according to human capacity. When Genesis says God created human beings male and female, this could be held to be the charter of the kind of essentialist binarism about sex that our biology no longer endorses. This may not, however, be the only or even best way to read Genesis 2.

Bearing in mind the ambiguities that surround sex, gender and coupling, Genesis 2:24 may not be legislating a rigid sexual order at all. The chapter is an aetiology, a narrative that explains why things are generally the way they seem to be. Genesis 2:24 marks human beings as male or female in a way that God himself is not. It may be most concerned to convey, not a biological theory that everyone is binary gendered and needs to marry, but a theological contention that the God of the Hebrews is different from almost all the other gods of the ancient world, who were firmly gendered in a way he is not.

Before any leaving and cleaving in Genesis, Adam and Eve's story says that God made people, by and large, with a radical and deep-seated need of companionship. This is the root of marriage in Genesis rather than the biological necessity of reproduction, gender difference or inheritance.

The Bible's grand narrative, indeed, is radically playful about inheritance. In much of the ancient world, and most of the time in Israel, legitimacy came from physical descent. The Bible legitimises people born out of turn and beyond their parents' capacity to conceive. The sequence that produced Jesus, logged in Matthew 1, contains women who radically fly in the face of conventional legitimacy. There is the adulteress Tamar, the prostitute Rahab, Ruth the Moabite, and even King David's stolen wife Bathsheba. Jesus' own ancestry is a moot point in St John's gospel, when members of the Judean establishment with whom he is arguing proclaim that, seemingly unlike him, 'we are not illegitimate children' (John 8:41).

St Paul, as apostle to the Gentiles, also plays fast and loose with physical inheritance in Galatians 4:21–31. He confronts the vexed question of who are the real children of Abraham by proclaiming that anyone who follows Abraham's faith in God belongs to Abraham's line, regardless of physical birth. At every point the greater purpose of God transcends the notional legitimacy conferred by marriage.

Same-sex marriage was, of course, unthinkable in first-century Palestine. Jesus' teaching about voluntary and involuntary eunuchs, however, pushes the envelope of strictly binary thinking about sex and marriage. People who believe the biblical doctrines of creation mandate medieval or Darwinian binarism about sex will find these verses deeply puzzling. Those who are willing to follow the logic of the way people seem to be made will think them well observed. Above all, they teach clearly that the way we are made sexually is more than strictly binary. Humanly speaking, the puzzles in our sexual make-up are insoluble. But, Jesus insists, with God all things are possible.

Another remarkable aspect of Jesus' teaching on marriage is the way he applies it to his disciples. Most religious communities, then and now, have strict and simple rules on the subject. Essenes could not marry. If you wanted to be a member of the Sanhedrin, you had to be married.

Jesus lays down no blanket policy for his disciples. Applying the general principle that rules were made for people not people for rules, marriage becomes a discretionary business, according to the individual's capacity. People should marry as they are personally willing and able.

Given the extent to which arranged marriages were the norm among the people to whom he was speaking, this teaching, obvious to us, has an undeniably radical edge in its original context. It also undermines any attempt to impose celibacy upon anyone against their nature, in the name of Christ.

Like Jesus in the gospels, St Paul believed that marriage was ultimately a personal and discretionary matter. The fact he had been a member of the Council implies that he should himself have been married. This is only a shred of indirect evidence for the notional existence of a Mrs Paul.

In general, St Paul's estimate of marriage is not entirely positive and, like Jesus, he sees the institution as belonging entirely to the present passing age. In 1 Corinthians 7 the apostle advises disciples, generally, not to marry. The world is ending soon and they have urgent work to do. They should not, however, burn with unrequited desire. It is very much a matter for personal discernment.

What is remarkable in St Paul's doctrine of marriage is how he eases the inequality between the partners that drove contemporary practice. For example, he advised both partners equally to yield to the other what he quaintly called their 'conjugal rights' (1

Corinthians 7:3). He sees the way married people belong to one another as mutual, but his general understanding of the way marriage partners should see one another remains hierarchical, like his view of slavery.

Thus St Paul, in Ephesians 5:21–33, instructs married Christians about the attitudes they should take towards each other and their marriages:

> Be subject to one another out of reverence for Christ.

> Wives, be subject to your husbands as you are to the Lord. For the husband is the head of the wife just as Christ is the head of the Church, the body of which he is the Saviour. Just as the Church is subject to Christ, so also wives ought to be, in everything, to their husbands.

> Husbands, love your wives, just as Christ loved the Church and gave himself up for her, in order to make her holy by cleansing her with the washing of water by the word, so as to present the Church to himself in splendour, without a spot or wrinkle or anything of the kind – yes, so that she may be holy and without blemish. In the same way, husbands should love their wives as they do their own bodies. He who loves his wife loves himself. For no one ever hates his own body, but he nourishes and tenderly cares for it, just as Christ does for the Church, because we are members of his body. 'For this reason a man will leave his father and mother and be joined to his wife, and the two will become one flesh.' This is a great mystery, and I am applying it to Christ and the Church. Each of you, however, should love his wife as himself, and a wife should respect her husband.

The Christian household mirrors the household of God. The apostle goes on to talk about the duties of parents and children and slaves and their owners. Most of what the passage says about marriage may seem unremarkable, like his guidance for parents and children at the beginning of chapter 6. Five verses later, in Ephesians 6:5, however, he reminds us that the first-century household belongs within the time-bound sociology of the age: 'Slaves, obey your earthly masters with fear and trembling, in singleness of heart, as you obey Christ.'

New Testament writers picture life in Christ in relation to all three of the great sociological realities of the ancient world, race, marriage and slavery. We have to interpret the significance of the concept of Christ married to his people alongside teaching that speaks of being grafted into a holy people by an inheritance that is more than descent according to the flesh, as well as aspirations to be 'a slave of Jesus Christ' (Galatians 1:10).

In all these instances it would be a fundamental misunderstanding of the matter to suppose they teach the necessity of the earthly institution as it was practised in the first century, far less that it could never be changed. All three had changed and were changing, and were to change radically, partly in the light of what he had written.

St Paul's instruction that husbands should love their wives probably seems obvious to modern readers of his letter. Many of its original readers might have been surprised to see love and marriage bracketed so closely together. Roman marriage was very much a matter of inheritance and property, often arranged by families. Slaves were not permitted to marry, not even other slaves, because allowing them to do so would compromise the property rights of their owners.

Ephesians refers back, as the gospels did, to the book of Genesis. It does this in the context of describing what it means to be fellow members of one body in Christ. In a sexualised culture it will seem that any reference to one flesh is entirely about sexual intercourse. For St Paul, unity within the body of Christ mirrors the unity he believes God wills between the partners to a marriage. This great mystery, as he terms it, is not about sex, but, as he suggests in 1 Corinthians 7, more about spiritual union.

Modern campaigners sometimes suggest that marriage can be defined by three basic realities which are not possible in a same-sex marriage – difference of gender, reproductive capacity, and a notionally natural pattern of sexual intercourse.

None of these three realities, however, can possibly play any role in the marriage of Christ and his Church. Christians do not all have to be female. They do not have to attempt reproduction for the marriage to be consummated, and any notion that the relationship is based on sexual intercourse between the parties is bizarre.

Marriage imagery in Ephesians is about the ordinance's deeper meanings, like structuring one's daily life within Christ's household, belonging to its owner as, in St Paul's first-century thinking, a wife does to her husband. In an age of dowries, the image carries an implication of having been bought with a price. If we take seriously St Paul's notion that marriage should be founded on love, being the bride of Christ sets self-giving love at the heart of the relationship. But any notion that the marriage is defined by sex, reproduction or gender difference makes the imagery absurd.

Bodily incorporation in Christ does not require a difference of gender, so it is hard to see how this can be held to be essential to becoming 'one flesh' in either Ephesians 5, Matthew 19 or Genesis 1. There is no need to over-sexualise interpretation of the terminology. It is about founding households, not having sex or children.

One other word in Ephesians 5:32 stands out for attention. The word 'mystery' in Greek becomes 'sacrament' in Latin. This fed naturally into the medieval idea of marriage as one of seven sacraments. What St Paul is talking about here however, is the mystical joining of Christ and his Church which is like a marriage.

This picks up and extends imagery of belonging to be found in Old Testament prophets, including Isaiah 54:4–8:

Do not fear, for you will not be ashamed;
do not be discouraged, for you will not suffer disgrace;
for you will forget the shame of your youth
and the disgrace of your widowhood
you will remember no more.

For your Maker is your husband,
the LORD of hosts is his name;
the Holy One of Israel is your Redeemer,
the God of the whole earth he is called.

For the LORD has called you
like a wife forsaken and grieved in spirit,
like the wife of a man's youth when she is cast off,
says your God.

For a brief moment I abandoned you,
but with great compassion I will gather you
In overflowing wrath for a moment
I hid my face from you,
but with everlasting love I will have compassion on you,
says the LORD, your Redeemer.

As with other biblical references to God marrying his people, this reference becomes ludicrous if its definition is assumed to require gender difference, sexual activity or the production of children.

It is about belonging, and finding identity within a social structure as strong as marriage in a clan-based society. Same-sex marriage would have been way off the social radar of the time and place, but there is no reason why the fullness of the reality behind this image could not be experienced within such a relationship.

Prophets in the Hebrew Scriptures use marriage imagery particularly to convey God's desire for faithfulness and permanence in his relationship with his people. A strong contrast is drawn between marriage, founded on permanence, faithfulness and stability and casual relationships with prostitutes, standing for idolatry and polytheism.

Thus God tells the prophet Hosea to marry a harlot, in order to demonstrate how it feels to have his bride, Israel, go whoring after strange gods. He will bring them back into a permanent covenant faithfulness, in which they will belong to him for ever:

> On that day, says the LORD, you will call me, 'My husband,' and no longer will you call me, 'My Baal.' For I will remove the names of the Baals from her mouth, and they shall be mentioned by name no more … I will take you for my wife forever. I will take you for my wife in righteousness and in justice, in steadfast love, and in mercy. I will take you for my wife in faithfulness; and you shall know the LORD.
>
> (Hosea 2:16–20)

On this basis the difference between married and unmarried states was not sex – concubines could provide that – but permanence. Christian thinking about this aspect of marriage led the way in the Middle Ages towards the doctrine of indissolubility.

A rather confusing passage, 1 Timothy 5:3–16, deals with widows. Losing a husband, a common enough occurrence in an age whose life expectancies were dramatically low by modern standards, reduced a woman's social position and deprived her of support in old age. Caring for the community's widows comprised a major part of early Christian charitable work.

In this context the passage says the Church should not be burdened by supporting widows who have children or grandchildren to support them. Young widows may marry again, but this should not be encouraged, for when they marry again 'they incur condemnation for having violated their first pledge' (5:12).

This could be just an observation about the risk of social disapproval a young widow might encounter when she remarried. It could hint at a marriage bond carrying on beyond the grave. But the hallmark of believers' marriages is to be permanence – a very important dimension to the unfolding history of Christian marriage. Like the covenant between God and his people, marriages between Christians should not be broken. On this basis the contemporary Jewish practice of divorce on (male) demand became radically questionable.

Rigorous ascetic movements grew within the Church as the apostolic age came to an end. The first letter to Timothy 4:3–5 rejects this path, warning against false teachers with seared consciences who forbid marriage and demand abstinence from foods, which God created to be received with thanksgiving by those who believe and know the truth. For everything created by God is good, and nothing is to be rejected, provided it is received with thanksgiving; for it is sanctified by God's word and by prayer.

Finally, the New Testament pictures the end of the age as a marriage feast (Revelation 21:2). As with other examples of biblical marriage imagery, any thoughts that it is defined by difference of gender, reproductive capacity or sexual behaviour is entirely absent. The passage teaches that the bride of Christ will, ultimately, be delivered to her spouse on the world's last day free of spot or wrinkle (echoing Ephesians 5:27).

Among last words in the Bible, Revelation 22:17 echoes Jesus' image of kingdom come as a marriage feast: 'The Spirit and the bride say, "Come!"'.

All biblical instances of marriage relate primarily to the times within which they were lived out. The order of polygamy and divorce on demand, which seems so natural in the period of David and Solomon, seems entirely anomalous in the light of the emerging desirability of monogamy and faithfulness in the evolving Bible tradition. The formally 'secular' institution, in the technical sense of the term, evolves according to the unfolding of the ages. It is rooted in the way people are created and its social meaning is defined contextually.

A notional single Bible doctrine of marriage can be constructed by making a judicious selection of texts and ignoring the whole picture. It can only be turned into normative dogma, however, by ignoring the basic fact that the definitions of marriage always come from lived experience of its realities, in the different social contexts of the Bible story. Among every age of Bible writers, the institution is defined from surrounding societies, including non-Jewish ones.

What shines through is that marriage in the Bible, in its various forms, is an externally defined social institution that is drawn upon to illustrate aspects of God's relationship with his people, about which regulations are made, but, more importantly, its spiritual and relational aspects developed beyond considerations of sex, gender or children.

The irresistible rise of Christian marriage

Marriage was set up and lived out variously in the cultural and historical contexts of the Bible. Jesus acknowledged it along with other cultural conventions of his age but did not, himself, marry. He was radically dispassionate about family loyalty. He rooted marriage not in its regulations, but the way human beings are created. He did not take the common view of his day that men were required to marry. Some should and could marry, others not, according to their capacity and inclination. Jesus taught that marriage was a formally secular matter – bound to each passing age in turn.

What have Jesus' followers made of sex and marriage in the light of his teaching? What have they thought they were doing when they married? How have their marriage definitions evolved with the passing of the ages?

Before exploring Christian marriage practice it helps to set the topic properly in its broad context. Father Timothy Radcliffe shrewdly observes:

> It is frequently asserted that Christians are obsessed with sex, and with what we are or are not forbidden to do. But for most of the last two thousand years, Christianity has neither been especially fixated on sex, nor has it thought about it in terms of rules. Jesus says little about sexual ethics, except on divorce. Nor was it a central concern in the Middle Ages. Think of the two great classics of Medieval Christendom, the *Summa Theologica* of Aquinas and Dante's *Divina Commedia*.

Thomas had a positive view of our passions, including sexual desire. They are basically sound and good. They can go a bit astray and need education and the purification of grace. But sexual passion is good, and belongs to our journey towards God, the one whom we most deeply desire. Aquinas hardly ever refers to the commandments. Sexual morality is about becoming virtuous, not about obeying rules.[1]

Bearing in mind this contextual health warning, Christian attitudes to marriage have undergone at least four developmental phases, the last two of which overlap:

- *Pre-endtime encumbrance* – 33–100 CE

- *Secular institution* – 100–1200 CE

- *Indissoluble sacrament* – 1200–

- *Partnership of equals* – 1650–

Pre-endtime encumbrance

The first Christianity was an apocalyptic movement. While there was nothing wrong with getting married, the end of the age was imminent. This left little time for marriage and family:

> To another [Jesus] said, 'Follow me.' But he said, 'Lord, first let me go and bury my father.' But Jesus said to him, 'Let the dead bury their own dead; but as for you, go and proclaim the kingdom of God.'
>
> Another said, 'I will follow you, Lord; but let me first say farewell to those at my home.' Jesus said to him, 'No one who puts a hand to the plough and looks back is fit for the kingdom of God.'
>
> (Luke 9:59–62)

It was better, however, to marry than burn with lust – an even greater distraction from kingdom business. St Paul acknowledged this, but taught that the urgency of the times was such that many committed disciples would, like him, pursue their vocation as free as possible from marriage and family responsibilities.

Christians did, of course, live in households. Sometimes this was as slaves who were generally not allowed to marry. Householders were exhorted to live exemplary lives, viewing their family relationships as places of witness to their faith.

Wives were to live in what may strike twenty-first-century readers as a rather 1950s' lifestyle that would impress the most demanding pagan husband:

> Wives, in the same way, accept the authority of your husbands, so that, even if some of them do not obey the word, they may be won over without a word by their wives' conduct, when they see the purity and reverence of your lives. Do not adorn yourselves outwardly by braiding your hair, and by wearing gold ornaments or fine clothing; rather, let your adornment be the inner self with the lasting beauty of a gentle and quiet spirit, which is very precious in God's sight. It was in this way long ago that the holy women who hoped in God used to adorn themselves by accepting the authority of their husbands. Thus Sarah obeyed Abraham and called him lord. You have become her daughters as long as you do what is good and never let fears alarm you.
>
> Husbands, in the same way, show consideration for your wives in your life together, paying honour to the woman as the weaker sex, since they too are also heirs of the gracious gift of life – so that nothing may hinder your prayers.
>
> (1 Peter 3:1–7)

Perhaps there were rather more Christian wives with non-Christian husbands than vice versa in first-century Rome.

Their instructions reflect the hierarchical way Roman marriage worked. This was slightly tweaked, by transferring to the husband some of the submission Roman wives were required to maintain towards their fathers, even after marriage. The watchword, however, was not to rock the boat. The Lord would do that when he returned.

Single Christians were urged not to be unequally yoked in marriage with unbelievers, but in an age when nuptials were largely an arrangement between families this was probably more of an aspiration than a target.

Most early converts who were married, inevitably, had spouses who were outsiders. St Paul's advice was that they should not separate, but rather lead home lives that might win their partners for the faith. He was realistic about the fact that Christian partners might be deserted by their spouses and should not, generally, be blamed when this happened.

Meanwhile, the Church pictured itself as a household within which authority was exercised along similar patriarchal lines to the secular order. God was pictured as a householder, with the Church his household. Widows occupied a special position within the Christian community as recipients of charity for whom the Church could function as family. Jesus had spoken of marriage as a permanent covenant grounded in creation, and early Christians pictured their relationship with God and one another in the light of this teaching. The end of the world was pictured as a startling and transcendent wedding feast to which the chosen would be rolling up soon.

Secular institution

As the first century drew to a close it began to dawn on Christians that Jesus might not be physically back soon. As this happened, Christian views of marriage entered a second phase that was to last over a thousand years. Christians were married and given in marriage exactly like everyone else. What this meant and how it was to be done naturally followed the conventions of the societies within which Christians found themselves.

The historian Philip Lyndon Reynolds describes the Church's attitude to marriage, which remained, at root, a secular institution:

> Christianity did not institute marriage but rather baptised it. In the early Church, converts who had been married before they were baptised became members of Christ's body as married persons, and by converting they committed themselves *ipso facto* to the Gospel's teaching on marriage. Similarly, Christians became married in the same way as their non-Christian neighbours did. In some respects, St Paul's approach to marriage was the same as his approach to slavery: he accepted the civil institution and the laws that defined it, but he explained how the Gospel required persons to behave within these relationships. As a secular institution, marriage was the subject of civil laws that determined who was qualified to marry whom and what were the conditions or criteria for valid marriage. In accepting the fact of marriage, the Church also accepted the secular rules.[2]

As time went by the Church acquired civil status and secular power. Christians also reflected theologically about marriage. Because it mirrored Christ's relationship with his Church, Christians tended to see the marriage bond as more permanent than their neighbours did. The difference between Christian and non-Christian marriages was to be found in the stability and permanence to which they aspired, not the nature of the bond itself.

St Augustine, fifth-century Bishop of Hippo Regis in North Africa, was, arguably, the first Christian theologian to value human desire in his theology. He came to Christianity through Manicheism, a Gnostic sect with a serious disapproval of sex that Augustine may never have quite escaped.

Augustine assumes that God made sex in order to continue the species, but this could happen without marriage. He himself fathered a child outside marriage and named him 'Gift of God'. Marriage brings legitimacy to inheritance, but this aspect is less important to him than its root – the core friendship that God instituted between Adam and Eve. He called this 'the first union of natural human fellowship', and it came before any sexual union or procreation.

Augustine taught that couples incapable of procreation were no less married than young bloods. Indeed, they could live closer to the heart of marriage, in deeper spiritual union: 'in good albeit aged marriage, even if the ardour of youth between a man and a woman has weathered, yet the order of charity between husband and wife thrives'.[3]

The idea that marriage's deepest aim was a profound relationship, not a means of procreation, flowed naturally from St Paul's teaching on spiritual union in 1 Corinthians 7 and Ephesians 5. Doing this echoed a trend outside the Church. Since the first century some Stoic writers began to speak of marriage as fundamentally a relationship rather than a civic duty or mechanism for procreation. Over the coming millennium, Christians baptised the secular institution of marriage, and their distinctively relational approach was to grow in importance until it was able, after the seventeenth century, to steal the show.

Throughout Christianity's first millennium it spread to new tribes and cultures, with their own takes on marriage and family life. As the Roman Empire broke up, new forms of society developed among Christians, many of which viewed celibacy as superior to conjugal life.

Jesus himself had implied that it was a noble thing to be a eunuch for the kingdom. From the beginning a few Christians, along with others influenced by Gnosticism, required sexual abstinence from their followers. New monastic movements developed and maintained a strand of Christian discipleship protesting against the world and all its works, including marriage.

Indissoluble sacrament

The thirteenth century saw a new way of reading the meaning of marriage in the Church. The Western Church began to make and control the institution of marriage in a tighter and more legalistic way.

People had begun to get married in church porches, with masses attached for well-to-do couples. The tendency was driven inexorably from the eleventh century by the growing habit of referring inheritance disputes to church courts. The Christianisation of marriage meant the church taking over the secular institution, synthesising Roman and Germanic law codes. The resulting Canon Law stressed the permanence of the covenant, while retaining the customary ease with which it could be made.

Throughout the Middle Ages, all that was required to marry was an exchange of vows that could take place anywhere. In May 1469, 19-year-old Margery Paston was dragged along by her mother and grandmother to appear personally before the Bishop of Norwich for marrying Richard Calle, the family bailiff. This was not only a moral failing but for a prosperous medieval family represented the loss of a valuable asset in the marriage market. The Bishop

> spoke to her right plainly and put her in remembrance of how she was born, what kind and friends she had and that she should have more if she were ruled and guided by them, and if she did not, what rebuke and shame and loss it should be to her.

Margery testified that she and Richard had indeed exchanged vows privately, and there was nothing more the bishop, her brother or her mother could do about it. Married to Richard she was, and the happy couple went on to have three sons.[4]

Divorce, however, was unthinkable. People say Henry VIII divorced, but of course no such thing was possible in England until over a century after his death. What Henry did was write his own annulment. Medieval Europeans who found themselves married to the wrong person had to prove there was some defect in the marriage. It could then be set aside. This was especially difficult, as Henry discovered, where major diplomatic and dynastic interests were driving the process.

It was easy to enter marriage but almost impossible to leave it. This made people increasingly careful about how marriages were made. It helped immensely for the vows to be witnessed by a priest, and as the Middle Ages progressed, increasingly formal ceremonies of bedding were developed for aristocrats and royalty, to prevent later disputes. Even so, Henry VIII affirmed strenuously what Catherine of Aragon fervently denied, that her marriage of a few months to his brother Arthur had ever been consummated.

The twelfth century had seen a remarkable reform of the Western Church. This tightened its grip over its members' lives and produced a new model theology of seven sacraments. Marriage became one. Its form was the exchange of vows symbolised by a ring. Its matter were the bodies of the participants. Its intention was their sacramental joining, demonstrated by the giving of consent to live together in the married state, sealed by a ring. The ministers of the sacrament, uniquely among the seven, were the couple themselves. The role of the priest was merely to witness and record the event.

As recently as the mid-eleventh century, William the Conqueror, known in the trade as 'William the Bastard', had been able to establish a claim to the duchy of Normandy by family consent, in spite of his birth out of wedlock. Very soon afterwards this would have been unthinkable, as ecclesiastical shutters came down on the world of marriage and personal morality. By the High Middle Ages the Church was well and truly in the marriage business, and formal liturgies developed accordingly.

In the early twelfth century Hugh of Saint Victor expressed a new theological implication of Christianising marriage. Its procreative aspect was a purely secular matter, for in life and theology children could be produced without the parents marrying. Hugh looked for his ideal to the chaste union of Joseph and Mary, ever virgin. This was his spiritual model for Christian marriage.

Hugh's tract *On the Virginity of the Blessed Virgin Mary* quotes Ephesians and Genesis and announces that the mystery it describes could only be possible with Christ if it is a spiritual union of two people into one soul, not a matter of mere carnality. Chastity was not the opposite but the highest form of married life:

> henceforth and for ever each shall be to the other as a same self in all sincere love, all careful solicitude, every kindness of affection, in constant compassion, unflagging consolation, and faithful devotedness ... In this way they shall dwell in the peace of a holy society and the communion of a sweet repose so that each no longer lives for self, but for the other. Such are the good things of marriage and the happiness of those who love chaste companionship.[5]

Hugh's ideal was Joseph and Mary. Procreation was a doleful necessity for young people, but the real work of marriage was chaste companionship. Hugh endorses heartily the Roman Jurist Ulpian's dictum that 'marriage is contracted by consent and not by consummation'.[6]

The idea that the highest form of marriage is celibacy seems strange, but Hugh insists that what best makes two people one is a union like the one in Ephesians 5, a spiritual mystery that unites two people's souls, rather than bodies: 'Is it possible for them to be companions of the soul,' asks Hugh, 'and not be holy?'

Sex played a very minor role, if any, in medieval *marriages blancs*. By the end of the twelfth century marriage was well and truly Christianised, that is, spiritualised. When the Church took over the secular institution of which Jesus had spoken it all but set aside pagan notions that its core meaning was about sex or fruitfulness. Its heart became indissolubility, founded on such mutuality of soul as Paul had taught in Ephesians 5. Pragmatically speaking, the Church also made itself the normal gatekeeper, referee and judge of marriage, exercising a new degree of power in the lives of its members.

Partnership of equals

As the Middle Ages drew to a close, the Renaissance saw new interest in the ancient fathers of the Church, including Augustine. Reformation liturgies, in languages understood by the people, articulated a concept of marriage as fundamentally a companionate personal relationship.

The English Prayer Books of 1549, 1551 and 1579 encapsulated and, in a way, democratised the institution of marriage. There was now a common vernacular form for making it.

Theologically, Cranmer's marriage liturgy reached behind the legalism of the Middle Ages, and rooted itself in the Bible and Augustine. It pictured marriage as a creation ordinance, adorned and beautified by Jesus at Cana of Galilee signifying the mystical union betwixt Christ and his Church. Cranmer drew from Augustine his concept of the goods of marriage. These were defences of it against those who believed celibacy was a superior spiritual state. They described not what marriage was – it was a secular institution – but three of its 'goods', or beneficial results. First, it provided a remedy against sin, St Paul's ancient alternative to burning with lust unto fornication. Secondly, it could produce children, though Cranmer was careful to proclaim the full validity of childless marriages by mentioning those 'past childbearing' in the prayers. Thirdly, it provided 'mutual society, help and comfort that the one ought to have of the other, both in prosperity and adversity'.

By the end of the sixteenth century, the Church had consolidated its hold over the institution by its liturgy, and its courts continued to rule over morals and marriages. The origins of marriage as a secular institution never entirely disappeared, however. Seventeenth-century marriages were as easy to enter as ever. The Church was only the witness not the maker of marriages.

The plot of John Webster's Tragedy, *The Duchess of Malfi*, written in 1612/13 turns on a secret marriage contracted without a priest:

DUCHESS   I have heard lawyers say,
                  a contract in a chamber
                  Per verba [*de*] *presenti* is absolute marriage.
                  [*She and* ANTONIO *kneel.*]
                  Bless, heaven, this sacred gordian
                  which let violence
                  Never untwine!

ANTONIO   And may our sweet affections,
                  like the spheres,
                  Be still in motion!

DUCHESS   Quickening, and make
                  The like soft music!

ANTONIO   That we may imitate the loving palms,
                  Best emblem of a peaceful marriage,
                  That never bore fruit, divided!

DUCHESS   What can the Church force more?

ANTONIO   That fortune may not know an accident,
               Either of joy or sorrow, to divide
               Our fixed wishes!

DUCHESS   How can the Church build faster?
               We now are man and wife,
               and 'tis the Church
               That must but echo this.[7]

This way of making a marriage was simple, to say the least, but it reflects from the other end of the Middle Ages that the heart of the matter is Hugh of St Victor's joining of souls. The Church could only echo the reality established by the parties outside its control.

All English social institutions underwent radical reappraisal during the mid-seventeenth century. As definitions of marriage evolved, the institution of divorce was rediscovered, not only from 'table and breast' but also 'from the bond' of formerly indissoluble marriage. The development was driven not by libertinism, but by Puritan reverence for the Old Testament and suspicion of Ecclesiastical control.

In 1612, Webster's Duchess had asked, 'Can the Church build faster?' The question was put with new urgency in the Commonwealth period. It found a radical answer from John Milton, who published four tracts on divorce between 1643 and 1645.

Coloured, perhaps, by his own rather chequered marital experience, but resting on close study of the Scriptures, Milton decided that the true meaning of marriage was not a sacrament mediated by the Church, but a companionate relationship. God had not primarily instituted marriage for breeding, nor sex, nor to delineate gender.

Milton focussed on Cranmer's third Good of marriage, 'mutual society, help and comfort'. Where this happened it would reflect the helpmeet relationship for which God had created Eve in the first place. Where it did not, as far as Milton was concerned, there was no marriage, morally speaking. Marriage was fundamentally a human reality, a meeting of minds, not an arrangement for sex or progeny:

> mariage is a human Society, and that all human society must proceed from the mind rather then the body, els it would be but a kind of animall or beastish meeting; if the mind therefore *cannot* have that due company by mariage, that it may reasonably and humanly desire, that mariage can be no human society, but a certain formality; or guilding over of little better then a brutish congresse, and so in very wisdome and purenesse to be dissolv'd.[8]

Merely formal or carnal union was eminently dissoluble. The way was potentially open now to marriage that was eminently dissolvable – as easy to leave as it had been to enter.

Milton protested that making marriage anything more than a loving relationship between two people was making it very much less. He railed against more complex sacramental and legalistic accretions that compromised the paramount Christian principle of love:

> Yet when I remember the little that our Saviour could prevail about this doctrine of Charity against the crabbed textuists of his time, I make no wonder, but rest confident that who so preferrs either Matrimony, or other Ordinance before the good of man and the plain exigence of Charity, let him professe Papist, or Protestant, or what he will, he is no better then a Pharise, And understands not the Gospel: whom as a misinterpreter of Christ I openly protest against; and provoke him to the trial of this truth before all the world.[9]

Legislative provision for divorce was delayed by the restoration, but could not now be stopped. By the end of the century aristocrats were freeing themselves legally from holy wedlock by private Act of Parliament. Among early beneficiaries was a Protestant blip in an ancient Catholic line, the 7th Duke of Norfolk, who divorced his wife Mary Mordaunt in 1700. The transaction did not serve him well, for after seven years of litigation he was ordered to repay £10,000 from his former wife's marriage settlement, had an apoplectic fit and died soon afterwards.[10]

The social effects of Civil War and Commonwealth were to relativise matters of religion, as well as spread new popular egalitarianism. This was expressed partly by new radical religious movements like the Society of Friends. Quakers were not alone in questioning the subordination of women within marriage defined by *couverture* that reduced them to items of property. In 1708 the Presbyterian minister of Chester, Matthew Henry, articulated a new sense of equality in his commentary on the creation of Eve:

> The woman was made of a rib out of the side of Adam; not made out of his head to rule over him, nor out of his feet to be trampled upon by him, but out of his side to be equal with him, under his arm to be protected, and near his heart to be beloved.[11]

Eighteenth-century English people were developing a more recognisably modern sense of themselves, reflected in the invention of the novel. In the world of the novel, marriage was almost entirely personal and relational.

At the same time, the burgeoning new English middle classes were developing their businesses and politics in a rational, bureaucratic direction. This required clarity about who was supposed to regard themselves as married to whom, and how, and what the legal implications were.

The most important eighteenth-century redefinition of marriage came with Lord Hardwicke's Act of 1753.[12] For the first time this required all marriages to take place in church, except for Quakers and Jews (but not Roman Catholics), where they would be registered after a ceremony that was made mandatory in England. During six days of furious debate, Henry Fox MP protested against the state usurping the power to invalidate marriages that were valid by both divine and moral laws. Such objections were, however, brushed aside.[13]

Lord Hardwicke's Act made the Church of England the formal maker of the vast majority of English marriages. It is understandable if twenty-first-century Anglicans feel that same-sex marriage legislation marks the final defeat in a long retreat from the position of almost complete pre-eminence the Church achieved in 1753.

This retreat happened by degrees and in slow stages. Early on Non conformists, then Roman Catholics, were allowed to marry in their own buildings as well as Quakers and Jews. In 1837 the government tightened up registration and certification procedures, but also, for the first time, became a maker of marriages for those who did not wish to get married in Church.

If civil registration undermined the status of the Church as almost sole proprietor of the sacrament, frontal assault came in 1859 with a new divorce Act that made marriage radically more dissoluble. To the horror of many High Anglicans, the State introduced a means of ending marriages that was open to those who could not afford a private Act of Parliament.

The motive was not to attack religion but to clean up an area of law that had become unacceptably messy in an increasingly tidy-minded age. Closing the means of divorce to the lower orders had not stopped some of them bolting informally. It was thought better that the State should know who was supposed to be living with whom than that the present mess continue.

As formal procedures changed, informal cultures about marriage were changing too. An increasingly mobile society was finding it harder to police its boundaries. Bride prices were becoming obsolete, and better-fed, longer-living Victorians began to enjoy increasing amounts of personal autonomy.

The main battleground over marriage for the Church of England was deceased wife's sister unions. These were against Canon Law, and an abomination according to Leviticus 18:18. The practice had not actually become illegal until 1842. Felicia Skene, writer and prison reformer, published an improving novel in 1849 called *The Inheritance of Evil: Or, the Consequence of Marrying a Deceased Wife's Sister.*

Victorians still drew marriage partners from a smaller circle of nearby candidates than has been the case since. A surprisingly large number of people felt inconvenienced enough by the ban to want it overturned. The painter Holman Hunt travelled to Switzerland after the death of his first wife Fanny, where it was legal for him to marry her sister Edith. Such a remedy was only open to those who could afford to travel.

The failure of a reform Act in 1842 inaugurated 70 years of guerrilla warfare between the Church and campaigners for reform, marked by failed bills in Parliament and raging controversy. Edward White Benson, Archbishop of Canterbury, was full of gloom about the prospects of losing a debate on this subject in June 1883:

> Arnold said, when the steam of the first locomotive passed Rugby, 'There is the death blow of the Feudal System.' This is the first real dissilience of the Law of England and the Law of the Church.[14]

When a Deceased Wife's Sister Marriage Bill eventually passed in 1907,[15] his successor Randall Davidson declared:

> For the first time in the history of the Church of England, has the law of the State been brought on one specific point into direct open, overt contrast with, and contradiction of,

the specific and divine law laid down in the authoritative regulations of the national Church.[16]

Lord Hugh Cecil, Highest of Anglicans as of Tories, was less diplomatic:

> I find it hard to believe that any person of Christian feeling or even civilised instincts can wish to inflict the sort of insult that would be involved in using our Churches and our services for carrying out what is in our conviction only an act of sexual vice.[17]

In the event, clergy were given a conscience clause. Soon enough thereafter the generation passed of those who reckoned such marriages were, in fact, abominations. It is doubtful many twenty-first-century clergy even realise they can decline to celebrate DWS marriages.

Why did the Church drag out what now appears a modest and sensible reform for over 70 years? Partly, the answer has to be that in those days it had more power to do so. Mainly, however, as the historian William Whyte has put it, those in favour of reform were disunited, while those against any change could play on all sorts of prejudice and fears.[18]

After 1907 the Church, in spite of much huffing and puffing about divorce following the First World War, was increasingly relegated to the sidelines. In 1937 an erstwhile Supreme Governor of the Church of England married a divorcee, and an American to boot. That year a new divorce act sailed through Parliament, giving women greater power to initiate proceedings and broadening the grounds of dissolution beyond those allowed by St Matthew.[19]

The game was now up for the medieval definition of marriage as indissoluble. What was arrived at was a classically English political compromise. In return for bishops in the House of Lords not blocking A. P. Herbert's bill, clergy were allowed for the first time to refuse outright to solemnise divorcees' marriages.

Hitherto they have been permitted to decline requests from couples involving a divorcee, but were required to find a colleague willing to officiate. Now at last, as the last shreds of indissolubility were being torn away in England, the clergy were finally entitled to behave as though it were as much a part of the definition of marriage as it had been 400 years before.

Honour was satisfied on both sides, but a chasm was opening between conceptions of marriage in Church and State. In 1938 beefy resolutions were rammed through the Church Assembly which, for the first time, instituted Lord Justice Penzance's definition of marriage from 1866 as Canon Law. By 1951 the Church of England was well on its way to having the canonical definition of marriage that its House of Bishops used in 2014 to try and disallow gay clergy from marrying.

The Church's concern throughout was not same-sex marriage, inconceivable before the 1990s, but divorce. In 1925 Cosmo Gordon Lang, then Archbishop of York, had called on the Church to ban the marriage of divorcees in order to stem the growing tide of divorce. The success of this strategy can be judged by comparing the divorce rate in 1925 with that in 1978, when the Church of England Synod retreated from this position, and admitted that there were circumstances in which the marriages of divorcees should be solemnised in church.

In the late 1930s the Church was narrowing its definition of marriage, while the State's understanding was expanding. Most churchmen took the abdication crisis as a victory, although the parliamentary story was actually one of defeat. The cultural influence of the Church remained strong, as Princess Margaret was to discover in 1955, when she withdrew from a plan to marry Group Captain Peter Townsend, a divorcee. The underlying trends in English society, however, were not favourable to the new marriage policy of the Church of England.

After 1945 English people who were not members of the Royal family displayed a greater tendency to divorce and remarry, partly because of the Second World War. This destabilised every social norm, uprooting young people, breaking up their families and, paradoxically perhaps, releasing many social constraints. Unsurprisingly, many wartime marriages did not work out and the divorce rate soared again with the return of peace. The more middle-class people obtained divorces, the more normal it appeared to do so, and social stigma was eased.

By far the most radical social influence on marriage in the middle years of the twentieth century, however, was the development of safe, cheap and female-controlled contraception.

In 1938 Church of England bishops had decided that there were circumstances under which family planning, as it was euphemistically called, could be allowable. This in itself implied that marriage was far more than sacramentalised reproduction.

Marriages are made by consent. It could be argued that by allowing intentionally non-reproductive marriages to be equal to reproductive ones, the Church embraced, probably more than it realised, John Milton's definition of marriage as a companionate state.

As the 1960s proceeded, not only did a safe, cheap contraceptive pill become available in Britain but, more significantly, it gave women control over reproduction without the indignities of former barrier methods. It finally broke the link between sex and procreation. This almost inevitably encouraged a greater degree of equality between the sexes. Social attitudes, as ever, lagged behind this development, but its importance is hard to exaggerate.

Breaking the necessary connection between married love and childbearing sent shudders up conventional spines. The Roman Catholic Church reacted by reasserting the link with its encyclical *Humana Vitae* (1966). Lay Catholics, especially middle-class ones, increasingly carried on regardless, and the encyclical failed to stem the use of the pill anywhere in the developed world.

In general, the ages at which people have got married rose significantly in the last half of the twentieth century. In a trend noted carefully by the Church of England's *Weddings Project* (2005), English people are now inclined to view getting married far less as the threshold of sexually active adulthood, and more as the crowning summit of a committed relationship.

Beyond the Church, ways out of marriage became easier in the last quarter of the century. The Church responded to this cultural and legal change by reassessing its hard line from 1957. After various committees and reports had examined the matter over 20 years, the Church formally acknowledged in 2002 what had always been the legal position, that discretion to officiate at a divorcee's wedding lay with the priest. It laid down new guidelines and a right of appeal to the bishop in case of disputes.

Most significant for the core definition of marriage, however, was a reform introduced at the beginning of the 1990s by a series of court judgements.[20] This brought to a final end the legal presumption since time immemorial that marriage contained within itself consent to sexual intercourse. Rape within marriage was now legally possible. Sir Matthew Hale had laid down in 1736 that 'the husband cannot be guilty of a rape committed by himself upon his lawful wife, for by their mutual matrimonial consent and contract the wife hath given herself up in this kind unto her husband which she cannot retract'. In 1991 consent to marry ceased to be a green light to sexual advances without additional consent. This radical limitation of what St Paul had called 'conjugal rights' did not in any way dilute the legal status of marriage, but redefined its core meaning.

Since the eighteenth century England has seen the rise and partial fall of rational bureaucratic State-registered marriage under the doctrine of couverture, sealed with a bride price. Multiple social redefinitions have been driven by ancillary laws about nationality, inheritance, social security and the means of forming marriages.

Beyond the complex and arguably personal world of marriage practice, the years since 1851 have seen four fundamental redefinitions. Wedlock no longer makes a woman her husband's property, is dissoluble at will, may be contracted against the laws of the book of Leviticus, and no longer contains in itself consent to sexual intercourse. Of course social evolution is by no means final. The year 2014 not only opened marriage to gay people, but finally criminalised arranged marriage, a practice with a pedigree going back to prehistory.

Marriage is not defined by Church or State, but by the lives of people who marry according to the social and personal mores of the time and place.

In other words, exactly as Jesus had said, marriage is fundamentally what it has always been – a matter of the present passing age.

Looking back over the past thousand years, where are we now? The medieval concept of marriage, indissoluble sacrament, has become a largely empty shell, even for many Roman Catholics. Meanwhile, the Puritan concept of it as a personal partnership of equals has stolen the show.

Geopolitics and mission

The biological phenomena that give rise to sexuality are universal. There are many different combinations of sexual identity and expression, but based on underlying biological structures shared by everyone. It can be no surprise, then, that behaviours and attitudes that could be described as homosexual occur all over the world, as they appear to have done in every human society hitherto.

Various sexualities, straight, gay and all points in between, express themselves in ways that are particular to each time and place. The spoken and implicit language of sex is seldom easily translatable. Any diversity officer in a modern multicultural university will testify how easily misunderstanding and misinterpretation occur between people with expectations formed in different cultures.

The contemporary world is contracting into a global village at an increasing pace. People are now communicating between and among each other instantaneously. New technologies have broken down the walls between different cultures and generations within those cultures. People in previous generations would have been unable to imagine the twenty-first-century volume or nature of real-time interaction.

This globalisation means there is now no hiding place. Fluid communications spread heat as well as light, misunderstanding as well as understanding. Therefore we know technologies do not always act as a homogenising force between societies. We can be sure, however, that there can be no return to the days of hermetically sealed cultural silos.

In the spring of 2013 the Pew Research Centre conducted a survey about attitudes to homosexuality in 39 countries, with over 37,000 respondents.[1] The only significant absentee was India, where polls were carried out but the results were not reported due to concerns about administration in the field.

The PRC survey revealed an amazing variety of different responses to the straightforward question, 'Should society accept homosexuality?'

The highest degrees of approval, over 80 per cent, were registered in Germany, Canada, Spain and the Czech Republic. The lowest, 2 per cent or under, were to be found in Tunisia, Pakistan and Nigeria. The most affirmative countries were to be found in Europe, North and South America, and Oceania. The least affirmative were concentrated in Africa, where the highest approval rating was South Africa with only 32 per cent, and the Middle East.

Making every allowance for the inevitable complications of language and culture that come with this subject, in 2013 people in different cultures saw this matter in radically polarised ways.

It is wise to be careful about drawing precise conclusions from the PRC survey. It seems that public acceptance is generally higher in more secular and affluent countries. It is generally lower in Africa and the Middle East. Attitudes at both ends of the spectrum show interesting local variations in volatility.

How gender-specific are attitudes to homosexuality? In most of the countries surveyed, views did not vary greatly between men and women. Interestingly, however, in countries with the largest gender gaps, women were considerably more likely than men to favour acceptance.

Generation was a major factor in the vast majority of countries surveyed, with every level of general public acceptance. Respondents aged 18 to 29 in almost every country surveyed were significantly more in favour than those over 50. The only exceptions were in sub-Saharan Africa. Ghana, Kenya, Senegal and South Africa followed the general pattern, but Nigeria and Uganda, with their microscopic public tolerance, showed higher acceptance rates among over 50s than under 30s.

The same survey investigated social change by comparing responses from 2013 to those generated by a smaller similar survey six years before. This comparison implied there had been a rapid process of acceptance since 2007, over 10 per cent, in South Korea, the United States and Canada. European and South American countries in which homosexuality is generally more tolerated registered lower increases between 5 per cent and 9 per cent. Intriguingly, Kenya's approval rate had risen from 3 per cent, in line with Nigeria's, to 8 per cent in 6 years – a significant rise, but against a background of massive public disapproval. Attitudes to gay people were broadly unchanged in the Middle East and Indonesia, but had hardened in the Czech Republic, Poland, Russia, the Palestinian territories and, intriguingly, France, which registered a fall from 83 per cent to 77 per cent.

Underlying these figures is a massive step-change of social outlook, especially in Europe and the Americas. Kwame Antony Appiah, the Ghanaian historian, has studied how moral revolutions happen.[2] By these he means sudden radical shifts of societal attitude towards well-established cultural practices. Customs like foot-binding in China and duelling in England very swiftly became dishonourable after they lost their social sanction.

From time immemorial right up to the turn of the nineteenth century, duelling was seen as an honourable way for gentlemen to settle their disputes. Something radical happened in the 1790s: it became unacceptable and soon afterwards illegal. In 1814 the last recorded duel in Wales was fought at Newcastle Emlyn. A Jamaican called Heslop was killed by Beynon, a local landowner, following a row about a barmaid's honour. The latter was found guilty of duelling and fined one shilling. By Victorian times, Mr Beynon would have been tried and probably hanged for murder.[3]

Appiah points out how swiftly these moral revolutions happen. Sentiment for a different way of seeing others builds up to a considerable degree of latency for change. Change itself comes from small minorities who articulate then enact a new social norm consistently. These resonate across wider society, especially among those whose formal practice has not yet changed, but whose way of seeing other people is untraditional. Once change comes, as the CIA used to say, you can't put the toothpaste back in the tube. Within a single generation, venerable attitudes that have held sway and commanded unquestioning obedience, sometimes over several thousand years, become obsolete as the energy that supported them turns out to have been exhausted.

This kind of realignment has happened within modern British society about a large number of social issues – slavery, religious intolerance, cruelty to animals, domestic violence, stigmas attached to illegitimacy, left-handedness and divorce, public displays of racism, limited electoral franchise, *droits de seigneur*, and violence towards children. The sudden wave of public revulsion following exposure of the entertainer Jimmy Savile and other 1960s and 70s TV icons as child and sex abusers shows how suddenly UK attitudes towards young people transformed between 1990 and 2010.

Increased acceptance of gay people is part of a much wider enlargement of the public mind and heart towards difference that came about during the twentieth century. The corresponding softening of public attitudes has not produced complete acceptance of women's equality, foreigners (especially those of visibly different races), or gays. It has, however, signally moved the goalposts in that direction. It remains to be seen how far a similar thaw in attitudes may or may not play out in other societies around the world as life in general becomes, hopefully, less brutal and basic.

What is certain is that attitudes to homosexuality have developed considerably around the world in recent years, sometimes by fits and starts. It could be that the rise of new generations and spread of global communications will induce similar developments even in what are now places of hardest intolerance.

That said, the second decade of the twenty-first century has seen new-model anti-gay legislation in Nigeria and Uganda. Support has been driven by a populist framing of homosexuality as 'un-African'. Politicians can easily sell this view to people who do not know their own history that well, and identify homosexuality exclusively with worlds of Western business and entertainment newly accessed on satellite TV and the internet.

The historical truth about this subject is very different. Generally speaking, indigenous African cultures were far more diverse and often very much more accommodating about gayness than the homophobic monoculture that colonial administrators imposed upon them. At least 21 cultural varieties of same-sex relationship flourished in traditional African life.[4] Christian missionaries recorded them, describing their first encounters with indigenous culture. These practices included female same-sex marriages among the Nandi and Kissi of Kenya, as well as the Igbo of Nigeria, the Nuer of Sudan and the Kuria of Tanzania.

Many forms of male homosexuality were recognised and flourished in the rich cultures of pre-colonial Africa. What Western imperialists, missionaries and colonial administrators imposed on Africa was not homosexuality, but their own intolerance of it, fortified by new legal provisions against it and incentives to suppress it.

In 1860 Lord Macaulay drafted a new law code to impose imperial discipline following India's First War of Independence, coining a new term for gay sex that would not make Queen Victoria blush – 'carnal intercourse against the order of nature'. This distinctive phrase, almost the only part of the British Empire on which the sun has yet to set, survives in the criminal codes of India and many former British colonies.[5]

This truth is very inconvenient to modern African politicians seeking scapegoats for the various ills of their countries.

Robert Mugabe has pursued gay people as vigorously as any African leader, using not only former colonial sodomy laws, but new regulations against holding hands or kissing. The jaws of people outside the political choir to which he preaches drop when they read denunciations like: 'Blair's government was not only colonial, but unnaturally stuffed with gay and lesbian ministers who were forced to marry each other.'[6]

No it wasn't

Perhaps the early twenty-first-century backlash against the West will blow over and, when it does authentic traditional African cultures may re-emerge. It may even be that British Christians, having vigorously exported their homophobia around their empire in the first place, could assume a special moral obligation to resource this aspect of decolonisation.

Homosexuality is still criminalised in 81 countries around the world. There are also some countries in the Middle East and Africa where persecution is increasing. It is a strange fact, but if one takes the list of countries in which Christians are most directly discriminated against and persecuted for their faith and compares it to a similar list where the same thing is done to gays, there is an almost eerie correspondence.

The real issue of persecution is not the particular community being persecuted, but the political and social circumstances that drive abuse in the first place. The big issues in such countries are the breakdown of civil society, violence, intolerance and disregard for basic human rights. Until these basics are addressed there is probably little point tinkering with the particular characteristics being victimised. The solution lies elsewhere.

What theological and missional consequences arise in a world where attitudes to homosexuality are intensely unstable and polarised?

There is a saying, often attributed to the great missiologist Max Warren, that 'It takes a whole world to know Christ.' The

Church is supposed to be the first fruits of a whole redeemed humanity. It cannot therefore confine itself to any monoculture, not even a churchy one.

The kingdom consists of what Revelation 7:9 calls

> a great multitude that no one could count, from every nation, from all tribes and peoples and languages, standing before the throne and before the Lamb, robed in white, with palm branches in their hands.

Prayers at Mattins and Evensong in the 1662 Book of Common Prayer spoke of God high and mighty, Lord of Lords, who beholds from his throne all dwellers upon earth. There is among them wide variety of cultures and polarised assumptions about sex, marriage and homosexuality. Everyone needs to acknowledge this reality.

Christians should not be spooked if mixing with other people's cultures is now unavoidable. The Church is a social and spiritual movement on a world scale – its Scriptures call it the rubbish of the world (1 Corinthians 4:13), while Jesus is seen as the firstborn of a whole new creation that is universal in its scope (Colossians 1:15). How, then, can Christians have any particular investment in homogenising cultures?

Everyone can now be aware of everyone else's lives in a way that has never been hitherto. All that goes on, including human rights violations in Sudan and marriage laws in the West, is interrelated on some level. Therefore, it is completely unrealistic, as well as contradicting the inherently cross-cultural nature of Christian mission, to expect everyone in the world to respond to the realities of the ways we are made sexually in the same way.

Every expression of Christian faith is contextual. The Church engages with people within their particular cultures, to incorporate them in a new humanity that transcends historic tribalism. Early Christians participated in the various marriage practices of the cultures from which they came. Some degree of understanding and respect for the integrity of different cultures will be necessary all round, within as broad parameters as possible.

Profoundly immersive openness to culture is not a concession to secularism. The incarnation requires it, and any workable paradigm for mission in the twenty-first century requires every Christian occasionally to suspend some of their disbelief about others on the far side of the world. David Bosch describes it in these terms:

> The missionary task is as coherent, broad, and deep as the need and exigencies of human life. Various international missionary conferences since the 1950s have formulated this as 'the whole Church bringing the whole gospel to the whole world.' People live in a series of integrated relationships; it is therefore indicative of a false anthropology and sociology to divorce the spiritual or the personal sphere from the material and the social.

> It follows from the above that mission is God's 'yes' to the world. When we speak about God, the world as the theatre of God's activity is already implied. God's love and attention directed primarily at the world and mission is 'participation in God's existence in the world.' In our time, God's yes to the world reveals itself, to a large extent, in the Churches' missionary engagement in respect of the realities of injustice, oppression, poverty, discrimination, and violence.[7]

Bosch goes on to say that mission is also God's 'no' to the world because

> what the Church proclaims and embodies in its mission and evangelism is not simply an affirmation of the best people can expect in this world by way of health, liberty, peace, and freedom from want. God's reign is more than human progress on the horizontal plane.[8]

Mission may not be a simple affirmation of the best people can expect in this world, but neither can the 'life in all abundance' that Jesus promised his disciples be any less. As a matter of fact, for many LGBTQI people, conventional Western Christian doctrines about sex and marriage amount to very much less – a world of deceit, fear and self-destructive duplicity. That is the obscenity of 'don't ask, don't tell'. The kingdom brings health, liberty, freedom and justice, not self-deception, duplicity and hand-wringing. By its fruits it is known.

Therefore Christians, while accepting other cultures for what they are, are in no position to suspend the life of the kingdom around them so as to collude with human rights abuses wherever they may occur.

The Archbishop of Canterbury found himself heavily criticised in April 2014 for a radio phone-in where he discussed a harrowing visit to the scene of an atrocity in Africa. Genocidists had claimed a right to slaughter innocent civilians to prevent them forcing the killers to become gay. In a subsequent interview with Cole Morton in the *Daily Telegraph*, he attempted to explain what he had meant. It was an atrocity.

> 'I've stood by a graveside in Africa of a group of Christians who'd been attacked because of something that had happened far, far away in America … and a lot of them had been killed.'

> That massacre was not in Bor, but he won't tell me where it is, for fear of endangering those who remain. The LBC host asked him whether he believed a Christian in Africa might suffer violence and abuse because of a decision made at Lambeth Palace about gay marriage? 'Yes,' he said. 'Precisely.'

> So in what sense was he misunderstood? 'What I said is that I have been in places where that has been the reason given for attacking people,' he says. 'Now, as I said then –

and this is where there was misinterpretation – that doesn't mean that you don't do certain things. That would just be giving in to that kind of terror.' To argue that you should not bless a gay marriage here just in case it might cause a killing over there would be a kind of moral blackmail, wouldn't it? 'It would be. You can't say, "We're not going to do X, which we think is right, because it will cause trouble." That's ridiculous.'

Instead, he is trying to acknowledge the need and suffering on each side and look through consultation for a way that will allow the Church to serve them both – however unlikely that may seem.[9]

Much criticism on both sides of the Atlantic arose from an impression that the Archbishop was, like the killers, somehow connecting the atrocity he had witnessed directly with Western liberalised attitudes. Gay people resented any insinuation that somehow they were responsible for the atrocities of African warlords. It was hard to believe that anything anyone did in the West would cause, or restrain, genocidal savagery.[10]

Yet it is true that Anglicans are singled out in some homophobic Muslim societies as members of a 'gay Church'. Bishops in countries like South Sudan experience real pressure on this account. Its basis, however, is so irrational that it is hard to know how anyone outside the situation can actually help.

What kind of dialogue could have been had with a virulent technician of the Nazi Holocaust? They would say that Jews were lice and vermin, holding Germany and the world to ransom according to the fictional *Protocols of the Elders of Zion* by controlling financial institutions. It is impossible to see how it would have helped anyone in that situation to pursue anti-Semitic discrimination in London or New York. The problem lay elsewhere.

We know, for example, that the Nigerian terrorist movement Boko Haram disapproves intensely of young women being educated. Their disapproval involves kidnapping innocent girls. Meanwhile we in the West believe that developing women's educational opportunities is a moral purpose. We have many fine institutions that pursue it. Would closing them down really moderate Boko Haram's behaviour?

There is also an aid dimension. When people in need say 'we cannot accept aid from people who differ from us on the gay issue', the tragic, toe-curling upshot is that they seem to have made a decision that has, sadly, to be respected. Aid will just have to be channelled through some other agency that values humanity above homophobia. If a Church really makes that choice, all it shows is how catastrophically homophobia impedes the work of the kingdom.

In the medium to long term the only answer to the harrowing atrocities of those parts of Africa where civil government has broken down is a robust reassertion of human rights. The Archbishop acknowledged clearly in his *Telegraph* interview that colluding with a moral blackmail would be as immoral as ineffective. If it worked it would validate a policy of atrocities. Thank God, then, that it wouldn't work anyway.

Most people in England do not set preserving the institutions of the Anglican Communion above justice. They are not, by and large, impressed by arguments that set keeping people happy above basic respect for human rights. If there really must be a choice between the two, the journalist Libby Purves is in no doubt as to which is the more urgent priority:

> The other common argument, as over gay clergy, is that the worldwide Anglican Communion would be torn apart by enraged African bishops if Western values overrode their homophobia. But if only prurience, cowardice and fudge can hold an institution together, is it worth it?[11]

The only alternative to this unattractive scenario is for Anglicans to find some way of living with their differences.

Archbishop Welby has made reconciliation and unity a great theme of his primacy. He has prioritised raising the Church's game about this. The Church will witness more powerfully to Jesus Christ if it can manage somehow to make itself a market leader in reconciliation rather than a notorious sink of inertia, evasion, duplicity, mendaciousness and hand-wringing.

Reconciliation has always been a major aspect of the Christian faith. St Paul saw Christians as people who were alienated from their neighbours and themselves, whom God has reconciled to himself and each other by the life, death and resurrection of Jesus Christ.

This could produce a powerful instinct to bring together people divided by the wraths and sorrows of the human race. The stories of the saints contain notable examples of peacemaking down to the present day. The Anglican Communion's newest martyrs, celebrated in Canterbury Cathedral at the 2008 Lambeth Conference, were seven members of the Melanesian brotherhood killed by warring factions while risking their lives to bring reconciliation in the Solomon Islands in 2003.

Christians' highest calling is to be reconciled reconcilers. This sometimes seems more of an aspiration than a target. Christians are also human beings, as subject to wrath and sorrow as anyone else. It makes them, at best, what Henri Nouwen called 'wounded healers'. G. K. Chesterton's 'Hymn for the Church Militant' (1922) captures the dilemma perfectly:

> Yea, we are mad as they are mad,
> Yea, we are blind as they are blind,
> Yea, we are very sick and sad
> Who bring good news to all mankind.

> The dreadful joy Thy Son has sent
> Is heavier than any care.

> We find, as Cain his punishment,
> Our pardon more than we can bear.

> Lord, when we cry Thee far and near
> And thunder through all lands unknown
> The gospel into every ear,
> Lord, let us not forget our own.

Reconciliation is a noble ideal that springs from the heart of Christian faith. Many people acknowledge its virtue, but are simply baffled that something as basic and culturally determined as attitudes to homosexuality, about which the creeds have nothing to say, and the Bible is all but silent, should give rise to irreconcilable difference between Christians.

Believers manage to disagree graciously about many profound moral issues – the taking of life in war, the eating of meat, the requirements of economic justice, forms of government and church government, sacraments. Why not homosexuality?

What used to be no more than a subject for seminarians' ethics essays has become for some the Great Shibboleth. Irreconcilable difference about it calls into question the Church's ability to offer reconciliation to the world. Archbishop Justin Welby has asked, rightly, 'How can we go around the world trying to talk about reconciliation . . . when we don't live it out in our own community?'[12]

One reason homosexuality has become the Church's flat tyre on its great pilgrimage comes from the nature of the question. Recognising gay people as the people they find themselves to be is very much a yes/no question. You cannot half-acknowledge someone else's full humanity as they understand it. Either you do or you do not. It's like pregnancy – you can't be a bit pregnant. In such questions there is no fence to sit on.

The sad fact is that a lifetime of steering round difficulties instead of confronting them has not prepared the Church of England for the situation in which it finds itself over gay people.

Bleating about what bad manners it is to name or face the issue, let alone solve it, compounds the difficulty. When people who are angry and helpless pretend not to be for years on end, it stokes up everyone's rage. The problem is not insoluble, but it can only be solved with the will to do so and a recognition that anything less than acceptance is non-acceptance.

What role is there for bishops? A bishop is called to be the focus of unity within their diocese. But what kind of unity, and how?

The kind of unity that is inherent in the Christian faith is reconciled brokenness stemming from the sacrifice of the cross, not bonhomie founded on ideological concord or institutional repression.

How can the head of a household promote family unity in the face of profound internal disagreement? Imagine a family at the time of the First World War with two young adult sons. One feels a strong urge, founded on his conscientious convictions about the circumstances in which they find themselves, to join up and defend King and country. The other feels an equally powerful urge, equally conscientiously, to be a pacifist and resist the war. What are good options for the lads' parents?

They can simply ban all family discussion of the war, hoping it will go away. As long as the strategy holds, it will make for temporary peace on the home front. This policy falls short, however, of taking either son's convictions seriously. It rests on moral cowardice about the real issues arising from the war. If something happens that presses the question, like a bomb through the roof or the death of the soldier son, the question will become unavoidable anyway, and the strategy will unravel.

Alternatively, the parents may allow their personal convictions to cloud their relationships with their sons. If they take the conventional view that the war is a great war to rescue civilisation from the Hun, they will congratulate the son who has joined up and offer him affirmation and support.

Doing this will implicitly belittle the pacifist son's convictions. He will experience this as exclusion. He will be told he is loved, of course, and accepted as a member of the family, but simply wrong about the war. Whatever the absolute rights and wrongs of the matter, the problem with this strategy is that it amounts to taking sides between the children. At the very least, the pacifist will experience disappointment at having to follow his conscience without his parents' understanding or support.

This strategy may be irresistible if the parents have very strong convictions about the war. Because it amounts to endorsing one son at the expense of the other, it cannot promote family unity. Whipping in Uncle Harry from down the road to have facilitated conversations with the pacifist son will actually promote disunity.

Wise parents who really want to live together in one family, whatever their personal view, will be willing to suspend judgement about any attitude that excludes either son. They need to understand what is really going on at home. They will allow each son to articulate his conviction according to his conscience, without playing one off against the other.

Even if they personally disagree with one of the boys, as will almost certainly be the case, they will not allow that consideration to cloud their judgement or diminish their respect for either son. They will take great care not to back either in a way that excludes the other. This is the only way they can be good parents to both their children and so maintain the highest level of genuine family unity in the circumstances.

The sad fact is that, whatever personal convictions the bishops of the Church of England hold, they have formally taken sides. Various listening exercises have been conducted over 30 years, designed to increase understanding and mutual respect. Unfortunately no one seems to have heard anything that would give them serious pause for thought about their dogma on this subject, shaped by a profoundly homophobic society. The sacred cows are safely grazing.

What gay people have heard is a strong message that says 'go and find out what the children are doing and tell them to stop'. Institutional cynicism reduces clergy same-sex marriages to a workplace misdemeanour, like thieving paperclips. Despair increases when bishops persecute and bully gay clergy who marry.

The cost of the unity for which bishops have appealed is continuing, out of inertia rather than intention, with discrimination that had to be tolerated back in the 1950s but does not any longer. In present circumstances, it steamrollers the conscience of the weaker party, whether it belongs to a member of the clergy who marries, or one who believes they are called to minister at a same-sex marriage.

Quite rightly, there is protection for conservative clergy who do not wish to officiate. It is scandalously abusive that while their convictions receive four levels of legal protection, those of clergy who see things differently are treated with contempt. The one-sidedness of this undermines and is unjust and morally indefensible. It is hardly surprising, then, that appeals to the status quo as unity have failed to impress those whom they exclude. Appeals to one-sided exclusivist unity have, in fact, radically increased the level of disunity.

We all have consciences, and respect for others is a cornerstone of civil society, as well as a requirement of loving your neighbour as yourself. There are limits, of course. If one person feels a conscientious duty to harm another, their exercise of conscience has to be limited so that as far as possible it leaves the other's human dignity unimpaired.

On this basis the Methodist Church in Great Britain has wisely decided to make the solemnisation of same-sex marriages a matter for local choice. Baptist Churches have held firm to the integrity of the local church in their ecclesiology and decided to do the same thing, in spite of most Baptists' strong objection to such unions.

The Anglican Church continues to mortgage the consciences of its members who believe they can and should marry same-sex partners to those of its members who believe others shouldn't be allowed to do such a thing. True unity cannot rest on violating the basic human dignity of one group of your own people to appease another. We are back to the bacon and eggs joke here.

How can the Church find true unity? Bishops do not have to agree with gay people who believe God is calling them to marriage, but if they have any sincere desire for unity they will have to enlarge their concept of it to take in married gay people. Unity in the Scriptures is a whole world redeemed in Christ. This will involve, embarrassingly perhaps, climbing down from their 1950s' high horse and being willing to take gay moral and conscientious arguments seriously.

Until this happens, the only kind of unity they represent will be narrow and stunted because it requires exclusion of the people with most at stake. No amount of window dressing, lather, hand-wringing, genteel lying, hiding under the desk, duplicity or euphemism can change this basic fact.

If bishops really want to be the focus of unity in our dioceses we will have to find courage to change. We are the stumbling-block, not gay people.

How can Christians around the world, starkly divided about how they interpret the ways they are created, live together? Bible arguments only help up to a point because pre-scientific or scientific definitions with which readers approach the text are radically incompatible. As was the case with issues like usury, the emancipation of women, capital punishment and slavery, all a narrow reading of the Bible can do is confirm people on both sides in their respective convictions.

Before giving in to despair, it may be worth considering resources that address this kind of division in the New Testament.

Early Christians were deeply divided over many issues that will seem incredibly basic to twenty-first-century counterparts. Do you have to be circumcised to be a Christian? How do you work out who is allowed to speak in worship? What role do the traditional food laws in your Scriptures have to play in your faith? What happens if you are married to an unbeliever who does not want to be married to you because of your faith?

Various competing answers arose in communities breaking new ground in their faith. Personalities figured largely in early Christian disputes, because at that phase of their development they relied heavily on charismatic leadership. They had not yet developed the institutional infrastructure to contain falling out with each other. What most of them did have, however, was vibrant faith, a clear vision, and the commitment to live together in a world that was often hostile or uncomprehending. What was necessary for survival was not to let the groups' personal dynamics steal the show.

Big divisive questions could not be evaded. There was no paper to cover the cracks. The major part of St Paul's teaching for the churches he founded involved clarifying the real underlying issues. There was no Christian centre or politburo. Credal formulations were embryonic.

The disciples did not respond to the precariousness of the situation, however, by pretending to be of one mind. Life in early churches was neither boring nor bland. Deep disagreement was passionate and pervasive. Thus on one occasion we find St Paul opposing St Peter to his face, calling him a hypocrite (Galatians 2). The Prince of the Apostles believed that Gentiles could be full members of the Church, but Paul perceived him to be simultaneously colluding with the narrow traditionalist party.

A big bone of contention was dietary laws. Without a doubt the Scriptures commanded them, and although Jesus had played fast and loose with the rules he himself generally observed them.

His teaching included two subversive principles, however. One was saying that the Sabbath was made for people and not people for the Sabbath. Another was saying the dirt that defiles comes from inside, not outside (Matthew 15:10–18). On this basis Jesus laid into the Pharisees for washing the outside of the cup but ignoring the inside.

At Joppa, St Peter saw a famous vision of non-kosher food descending in a blanket (Acts 11:2–10). God had warned him not to call unclean those things he had created to be received with thanksgiving. The first Council of Jerusalem in Acts 15 did enforce the principle of kosher killing, however. Like other official decisions, it does not look as though this line significantly outlasted the end of the Council.

Two larger arguments made food observance critical. One was the question of circumcision, and the status it conferred on Christian believers, or not. The sign was the distinctive mark of the Jewish male, and there were parties among the early Christians who were not willing to surrender this Bible principle lightly.

For Gentile converts as well as for Jews, food became particularly explosive ammunition because of its association with idolatry. Idolatry was the worst sin in the book. The first commandment left no room for doubt about this. Rigid monotheism was a distinguishing factor of synagogue and church in a society with many gods. As Paul the apostle walked around the streets of Athens, he noticed its huge profusion of temples to gods from all over the world, known and unknown. Polytheism was so pervasive that some of St Paul's first hearers in Athens thought he had come to bring them two additional gods, Jesus and Anastasis (the Resurrection) (Acts 17:18).

Idolatry, then, was a major issue for Christians. When 1 John 5:21 urged early Christians to keep themselves from idols it was warning them off a very real and pervasive peril. The cutting edge of this issue was whether Christians were or were not vegetarians. This caused profound division among them.

Why in particular?

There was, in fact, no non-religious source of meat. The only way to be absolutely sure of not 'partaking at the table of Demons', as St Paul pictured it, was to be a vegetarian. It was in some ways the most obvious policy. By refusing meat Christians could avoid any kind of impurity that might arise from its origin. They could also ensure that their money was not supporting pagan priests in any way, shape or form. Becoming a vegetarian was a principled stand, to defend the heart of Christian discipleship.

Feelings ran high, certainly on the rigorist side. Revelation 2:20–23 makes it plain this was still a salvation issue in the church at Thyatira at the end of the apostolic age:

> I have this against you: you tolerate that woman Jezebel, who calls herself a prophet and is teaching and beguiling my servants to practise fornication and to eat food sacrificed to idols. I gave her time to repent, but she refuses to repent of her fornication. Beware, I am throwing her on a bed, and those who commit adultery with her I am throwing into great distress, unless they repent of her doings; and I will strike her children dead.

Another faction of believers, however, took a very different line on meat. Had not the Lord himself said that real impurity flowed out of people's corrupt hearts, not into them from what was, when all was said and done, dead meat? Thus the Lord 'declared all foods clean', said St Mark (7:19), though some other early Christians may not have drawn exactly this conclusion.

In the old dispensation, purity and ritual taboo had been an important way of setting God's holy people apart from the world. In the light of the Lord's teaching, a new freedom had dawned. Gentile converts, having been excused the basic requirement of circumcision, found it hard to see why they should obey mere food laws. As for ritual pollution, if Christ was all and in all, the fact could be demonstrated by eating meat regardless of its origins. Christians could eat at the table of demons with impunity because of Christ's supremacy over all pagan gods. Doing it signified faith in his primacy over all.

This dispute produced two bitterly opposed factions within the Church, both professing that Jesus was Lord, but with radically incompatible ways of expressing it. Feelings seem to have run high.

The vegetarians accused the carnivores of laxity and indifference. All they wanted to do, their enemies insisted, was not stand out at pagan dinner parties. They were conforming to the way of the world about idolatry, a basic gospel issue.

The carnivores accused the vegetarians of rigourism. Why should those who had been set free under the new covenant behave as though they were still shackled by old purity laws that were powerless to save them anyway?

St Paul's letters contained ammunition for both sides. His letter to the Galatians (3:29) affirmed the importance of following Abraham's attitude and deeds, so that Christians could make up by faith what they lacked in physical descent. But the same letter waxed strong against a circumcision party for trying to bind Christian conscience to the letter of the old law. Its teachers were described as 'false brothers, come to spy out the freedom that we have in Christ' (2:4). For freedom Christ had set Christians free. They were never again to surrender to a yoke of slavery (5:1).

Towards the end of his letter to the Romans St Paul addresses this profound division. Having explored in detail the universal nature of sin, and the completeness of the forgiveness by grace through faith, he turns to the kinds of living status that go with being 'in Christ'. Love is its theme. The letter of the law is all very well as far as it goes, but God has accomplished in Christ something that the law, weakened by sin, never could (Romans 8:3). Therefore any particular ordinance, even such basics as the Ten Commandments, could be briefly comprehended in loving one's neighbour as oneself (Romans 13:10).

In chapter 14 St Paul addresses the issue of factionalism about meat. Many church leaders might have tried to take the heat out of the issue by compromise or an appeal to the status quo. Paul does not command either party to cease and desist. Quite the reverse. Failing to act on faith is a bigger sin than getting the particular issue wrong. Therefore, Paul orders both sides to act out their convictions to the hilt, but be mindful of the others:

> Those who eat must not despise those who abstain, and those who abstain must not pass judgment on those who eat; for God has welcomed them. Who are you to pass judgment on servants of another? It is before their own lord that they stand or fall ... Let all be fully convinced in their own minds.

> Let us then pursue what makes for peace and for mutual upbuilding. Do not, for the sake of food, destroy the work of God. Everything is indeed clean, but it is wrong for you to make others fall by what you eat; it is good not to eat meat or drink wine or do anything that makes your brother or sister stumble. The faith that you have, have as your own conviction before God. Blessed are those who have no reason to condemn themselves because of what they approve. But those who have doubts are condemned if they eat, because they do not act from faith; for whatever does not proceed from faith is sin.

> (Romans 14:3–23)

European and African Churches have taken this kind of approach in modern times to marriage doctrine.

Some African societies are systemically polygamous. Yoruba culture, for example, measures the status of its men by the numbers of their wives. This is not, for them, libertinism, but the structure of society. Christian missionaries reacted to this fact in various ways. Early pioneers on the Niger Delta noted the custom, were horrified by it, and attempted to stamp it out by banning converts from multiple marriages.

Some missionaries gave the first wife primacy. Roman Catholics allowed men to choose a favourite wife to be regarded as the real one. Other missionary thinkers, including Adrian Hastings, after service as a White Father in Uganda, began to consider in the 1970s that there might be a way to live with the culture on its own terms. Eventual resolution would emerge from Christian communities following the principles laid down in Romans 14. If, as he believed, any form of polygamy was a bad development God would iron it out in due course. In the meantime division over marriage practice should not be allowed to destroy the possibility of a genuinely indigenous Church emerging within African cultures. Better that than pretend, as was often happening on Protestant missions.

Jon Kuhrt has shown how important it is to healthy Christianity not to homogenise the community. By allowing variety to flourish, the Church transcends what he calls 'Tribal Theology'. In England this would include going beyond the usual boring old punch-up between Western conservatives and liberals, much of which just boils down to anxiety, or lack of it, about change:

> creative tensions abound in Christianity. At heart of our faith is the belief that an eternal, omnipresent God incarnated Himself into a specific space and time within human history. We believe that God is both transcendent, wholly other from creation – but also immanent, a God who we can know as a Father. We believe in both experience of God's grace working in our lives and in a revealed truth in the Bible. We believe in both a personal encounter of Christ and the social witness that the Church is called to live out. We believe in both the truth of the incarnation of God in Christ and the atonement that he brought about through his death. To all of these aspects of theological truth, the orthodox Christian can say 'I believe'.

> It is this dialectical nature of truth that is Christianity's strength in being able to engage with the real world. It is

rooted in the rabbinic tradition in which Jesus' ministry was birthed – where dialectical instructions, for example, to be 'wise as serpents and innocent as doves', were common.

Grappling with the dialectics such as these is central to what it means to be part of the Body of Christ.[13]

If this is true, a Church that engages fully in life, but openly and honestly, is a better Church for containing internal differences that matter. God allows shibboleth issues to develop, partly to give Christians an opportunity to love their enemy within the household of faith, and partly, as Paul puts it in 1 Corinthians 11:19, because 'there have to be factions among you, for only so will it become clear who among you are genuine'.

This does not make factionalism a good thing, more a fact of life, but the more a Romans 14 approach is applied, literally, to Churches in their various cultural contexts, the more it could be possible for them to be agents of mutual understanding and reconciliation rather than creating hate and alienation between themselves.

The only thing that truly surprises people missionally is love with open eyes. A Church that only half-heartedly affirms love hobbles its own mission. Boycotts and walkouts simply reflect the characteristic tactics of a divided world, and apply political solutions to what is ultimately a spiritual problem. Honest disagreement that takes everyone as seriously as everyone else can transcend any particular culture and offer hope to a world in sore and increasing need of reconciliation and healing.

9

'The law of the land, and that's great'

A few seconds after midnight on 29 March 2014, at Islington Town Hall, the balloon went up. Messrs Peter McGraith and David Cabreza made Britain's first same-sex marriage. Moments later at Brighton's Royal Pavilion, Neil Allard married Andrew Wale and said he found the ceremony 'much more moving' than expected:

> 'We were considering a civil partnership, even though we didn't think it was true equality, so we're very, very happy that this day has come, finally.'[1]

The Prime Minster declared it 'an important moment for our country. It says we are a country that will continue to honour its proud traditions of respect, tolerance and equal worth.'[2]

Others predicted altogether more dire consequences. David Sylvester, a councillor in Henley-on-Thames, pronounced the recent bad weather God's judgement against gay marriage:

> Since the passage of the Marriage [Same Sex Couples] Act, the nation has been beset by serious storms and floods. One recent one caused the worst flooding for 60 years. The Christmas floods were the worst in 127 years. Is this just 'global warming' or is there something more serious at work? The Scriptures make it abundantly clear that a Christian nation that abandons its faith and acts contrary to the Gospel (and in naked breach of a coronation oath)

will be beset by natural disasters such as storms, disease, pestilence and war.[3]

But even worse might follow. Pastor Enoch Adeboye of the redeemed Christian Church of God (Lagos), warned that same-sex marriage would wipe out the entire human race within 20 years:

> How can a man who marries a fellow man produce a child? How can a woman who marries a woman produce a child? If this evil is allowed to stay there will not be newborn babies again in the world. As the older generation dies, would there be new generation to succeed them? Even plants and animals have new generation to succeed them![4]

Reactions from mainline British Churches were more muted. The Archbishop of Canterbury put out a statement saying he accepted that the law had changed – a sentiment that provoked negative response in conservative circles as he told *Pink News*:

> As you know I have said, and got a fair amount of flak for it within parts of the Church, we have to accept, and quite rightly, that the same-sex marriage act is law, and that it's right and proper, it's the law of the land, and that's great.[5]

Soon afterwards, Lambeth Palace rushed out a clarification. The Archbishop had not meant to suggest that gay people marrying was great, simply the fact that Parliament had been able to change the law.

Laying aside hyperbole and hand-wringing, what kind of a future will come from gay people marrying?

LGBTQI people form only a small minority of the population. It could be expected that in the ten years following legalisation many thousands of couples in Britain will enter same-sex marriages. A small early bulge is inevitable, but not as large as it was for civil partnerships, being paced somewhat by delay in implementing the procedure for converting civil partnerships into marriages.

For many entering same-sex marriages, it gives legal endorsement to a relationship within which they have lived for a very long time. This high degree of latency means nothing much will change at street level – at most a tiny social earthquake, with no injuries likely.

A substantial minority of same-sex marriages can be expected to fail, however, exactly as with other marriages. Others will take deep root, bear fruit, found households and grow into profound and nourishing relationships that enrich community and strengthen the social bonds at the heart of society.

The headline concern of those protesting against the change has been sex. So will gay sexual activity increase?

All marriages involve varying levels of sexual activity during their courses. Various anxious Christians have expressed the fear that recognising gay people's relationships as marriages will increase the amount of anal sex that goes on.

Research into sexual behaviour is notoriously difficult and specific to particular cultures, but tentative figures are available from the USA. These indicate that around 34 per cent of gay people practise anal sex, while 40 per cent of straight people do. If these figures were reproduced in the UK, we could expect that over ten times as much anal sex goes on between straight couples as gay.[6]

Therefore, those who have a mission to put a stop to this kind of thing would do best to focus their efforts on the overwhelming number of anal sex practitioners who are straight. Furthermore, as a matter of fact, it has to be very questionable to characterise gay people by a form of sexual behaviour which a higher proportion of straight people practise anyway. This number could amount to 100 million more in the USA alone.

What else may follow the advent of same-sex marriage? Conventional wisdom indicates that marriage encourages sexual fidelity while inability to marry encourages promiscuity. It is possible, then, that marginally less promiscuous sex will go on in Britain.

Finally, we can assure Pastor Adeboye, the human race will probably exist in 20 years' time. If it does not, it is hard to see how the fault will lie with LGTBQI people for having married.

What social impact will same-sex marriage have?

The rhetoric of those who campaigned against same-sex marriage could soon seem as curious as that of Dionysius Lardner in the 1840s. He believed that if a train's brakes failed in Box tunnel it would accelerate to 120 mph, break up, and kill all the passengers. Lardner had not taken into account air resistance or friction. These have their social equivalents. Society tends to cushion and normalise the most extreme effects of relationships. The story of massive social change in Britain since 1945 about race, class and the position of children indicates that fear and fantasy tends to crumble in the face of real experience.

As long as LGTBQI people were effectively excluded from marriage, it was possible to argue against a change in the law while claiming this said nothing about the nice gay couple next door. Once that couple is married, this claim collapses. People will draw their own conclusions about whom they consider to be married and whom they do not, as they always did.

A minority of people will continue to believe that same-sex marriage is impossible. They are free to do so. This conviction could end up roughly as countercultural as creationism. The people who hold to it will feel the satisfactions of being a self-righteous minority that few will begrudge them. A broadly tolerant society will accept that that is the way some people feel, and best of luck to them.

There is a particular danger for Churches. Those who persist in side-lining, stigmatising and even threatening their gay ministers are in danger of making themselves the only places left in society where this kind of behaviour goes on. The only way to reverse such ghettoisation would be serious internal work to address the Church's institutional homophobia. In the year of legalisation it is, to put it kindly, very questionable whether any serious will to do this exists, let alone understanding of how it might be done. What can be said is that as long as naming the existence of the problem is officially stigmatised as bad manners, the institution is kidding itself if it thinks it has got out of the starting gate.

During the arguments over same-sex marriage, it was sometimes suggested that allowing gay people to marry would cheapen the meaning of marriage for everyone. At one point, the archbishops of the Church of England spoke of LGTBQI marriage 'diluting' the institution.[7] They did not explain quite how this would happen.

What exactly is it about gay people that cheapens other people's lives or dilutes their marriages? No one in authority seemed to be able to say. Articulating the notion more clearly would involve explaining how gay people, simply by being the way they are, diminish rather than enrich marriage. It is hard to see how the notion could be expressed without sounding a crude, homophobic note that church authorities would rather not be caught expressing in public.

Far more positively, and alone among English diocesan bishops at the time, the Bishop of Salisbury wrote, stating what to most people was obvious, that :

> The possibility of 'gay marriage' does not detract from heterosexual marriage unless we think that homosexuality is a choice rather than the given identity of a minority of people. Indeed the development of marriage for same-sex couples is a very strong endorsement of the institution of marriage.[8]

How, then, might same-sex marriage enrich the institution?

First and most obviously, expanding the range of people able to marry brings a broader diversity of experience, conviction and proclivity to the way that the institution works in society. A greater degree of openness, honesty and self-awareness (with less hypocrisy, fear and self-deception) about sexual identity is healthy.

It is often said by sociologists and educators that there are many kinds of different family in modern Britain. Allowing gay people to marry legally brings the traditional social endorsement of marriage to people who, only a generation before, had been treated as deviants. Many LGBTQI people will not choose to marry, as many straight people don't, but the right to do so if they choose to remains significant.

Secondly, expanding the bandwidth of marriage demonstrates the resilience of an institution that had seemed to many hidebound and irrelevant. In January 2013 the Very Revd Peter Atkinson, Dean of Worcester, drew attention to marriage's resilience. He pointed out that 'If marriage is an "institution" at all, it is one with a built-in faculty for re-inventing itself'.[9]

Many baby-boomers fought shy of marriage in the last quarter of the twentieth century because it seemed to be an inherently unequal and patriarchal form of conventional living. Many cohabited instead, because they valued a partnership of equals, more than a dynastic arrangement or a licence for sex that they were having anyway.

The possibility of two women being married to each other and working out this status in their lives, in itself, challenges the necessity of patriarchy for marriage. Legal recognition of marital rape, like the opening of marriage to all sexual orientations, breaks the link between marriage, inequality and patriarchy, at a fundamental level. By doing so, it opens up a broader future for the institution. John Milton would be pleased.

Thirdly, far from fulfilling pastor Adeboye's fears that same-sex marriage would destroy the next generation, it creates new married households, founded by same-sex couples, within which children can find status and security in the same way as in other households. It secures rights of residency, inheritance and guardianship. Marriage does not figure as significantly in British social security provision as in the USA, but household legitimacy remains a solid gain arising from opening marriage to LGBTQI people. As there are more same-sex married families around the world, evidence is beginning to stack up that children do as well, or even better, in them than in heterosexual ones. These are early days, however, and same-sex couples make up such a tiny proportion of the whole number of marriages that evidence about this at the moment is scant and hard to assess.

Fourthly, allowing same-sex marriages removes the anomaly by which gay people used sometimes to marry an opposite-sex partner in the hope it would straighten them out. As recently as the 1970s, well-meaning elders encouraged this abuse of marriage as corrective therapy for gay people. One or two happy or fruitful marriages resulted (particularly if bisexual people and their partners were willing to accept each other as they were) but this strategy was doomed in its own terms, and responsible for much misery and psychological damage. Doing away with this anomaly strengthens the institution of marriage from within.

Fifthly, and in some ways most significantly, wholeheartedly affirming same-sex marriages gives social recognition that reverses centuries of stigmatisation and shame. A Church that found it in its heart to practise equality like this would be baptising a culture that many Christians fear and resist, in exactly the same way as the medieval Church baptised the cultures in which it flourished, including their marriage customs.

As long as LGBTQI people were stigmatised as a deviant minority defined by their supposed sexual behaviour, allowing them to marry was unnatural. The same things were said about inter-racial marriage back in the 1960s and 70s. Now social imagination has enlarged in relation to minorities and racial groups, society has chosen to see diversity as natural — a strength not a weakness. Distinguishing characteristics of any particular minority become a source of positive enrichment rather than negative threat.

What implications are there for the Church?

The Church could wholeheartedly accept same-sex marriage, with the same opt-out conscience clauses for clergy as they currently have for divorcees and deceased wife's sisters. Some benefits of this can be cast in terms of Niebuhr's 1951 categories for understanding Christ and culture:

- *Christ against culture* – A Church that holds same-sex marriages in honour is free to confront homophobia in the UK and around the world, by challenging its mostly religious roots from within.

- *Christ of culture* – By accepting same-sex marriage, a Church reasserts its traditional view that the heart of marriage is spiritual union not breeding. This brings the freedom to live out more fully the logic of the incarnation in the twenty-first century.

- *Christ above culture* – God is love and those who live in love live in God and God lives in them, whoever they are. This is the Good News, not cultural containment within the social prejudices of the past.

- *Christ and culture in paradox* – Since same-sex marriage is as countercultural in Nigeria as it is cultural in Spain, the worldwide Church can only live out the catholic aspect of its character on the basis laid down in Romans 14. Taking the coexistence of incompatible views as an opportunity not a threat lets each Christian be convinced in their own mind and turns gay scapegoats into sisters and brothers. This demonstrates an enduring power of the cross to bring healing and hope.

- *Christ transforming culture* – When Churches surrender the unhistorical notion that marriage was ever a fixed reality, they can participate wholeheartedly again in its development. It becomes a point of contact with, rather than alienation from, the whole community. The Church of England's Weddings Project has shown the great missional value of engaging fully in the world of contemporary marriage, not holding aloof from it.

Given the vast range of attitudes to the phenomenon of homosexuality around the world, thus the worldwide family of Churches, the only proper line any Church can take about other Churches' missional engagement with their cultures is pragmatic (if provisional) acceptance founded on equality. Each must be convinced in their own mind.

Niebuhr's categories only engage with the possible implications of doctrine in particular social contexts. Churches also have to engage with the truth at the heart of the matter. Scientists have developed concepts of biology and sexual orientation in response to the reality they study. If the almost universal thrust of their conclusions is correct, it cannot be right to punish gay people any more for being as they are, whatever our grandparents' cultural dictates would have been.

This appears to be the heart of the matter. Sorting through an extensive postbag on the subject of same-sex marriage, there are two incompatible kinds of response.

The first sees sex as a simple binary characteristic, with heterosexual behaviour to produce babies as the only truly natural form of sexual desire or expression. All Bible texts are then interpreted according to this foundational assumption.

A second view sees the way that human beings are made differently. Sexualities arise from where their owners belong on various scales, with considerable variation. Biological sex is not simply binary, but a biological characteristic that takes in a variety of sexual and intersex possibilities. Gender is an awareness of maleness or femaleness with which people identify. Orientation, a matter of the heart, is a matter of sexual attraction, which in itself is variable, including a tiny minority whose orientation is asexual. Sexuality is expressed in a sociological context with a shared gender identity for the framework within which people interpret sexual and gender expression. God has made everyone fearfully and wonderfully, and moral responsibility arises only from the choices that they consciously make, mostly in the area of sexual behaviour. Therefore it is as natural to be gay as straight.

These two views are incompatible. They are matters of definition. They are not founded on theology; therefore the difference between them cannot be resolved by theology. Many theological positions can be held alongside either of them, but on a definitional level whichever of these positions is taken will determine the way the Bible is read.

Natural theology develops according to human understanding of nature. Many Victorian Christians thought the book of Genesis was reportage. As the nineteenth century progressed, geologists, as much as biologists, increasingly challenged that interpretation. The world suddenly seemed to be very much older than 4004 BC.

Some Christians saw the fossil record as a deliberately misleading decoy God planted to fool the faithless. Most Christians did not, however, and after 150 years they have made their peace with the theory of evolution. Meanwhile, constructive theologians like Teilhard de Chardin have taken the concept of evolution as the basis for a new kind of theology.

The theory of evolution can still be contested, especially some of its finer details, but the broad drift of science on the subject of human origins is pretty much settled. We will not awaken one day to find ourselves back in the 1830s, with evolution no more than a bad dream.

In a very similar way, the basic science of sexuality has room for experimental research of many kinds, but we will not be returning to the simple binary certainties of our grandparents about this subject. The science is pretty much nailed.

The beginning of same-sex marriage posed three questions for the Church of England, two acute, and one chronic and more important.

Most immediately, how is it going to respond to demand for same-sex marriages? This question has suddenly ceased to be academic. Patrician hand-wringing about homosexuality used to seem rather wise and grand. It no longer does. Having an increasing number of gay married couples in society makes it seems foolish and evasive. Pressure will only increase with passing time. Devising blessings where nothing is blessed will be as difficult as coming up with a low-alcohol whisky, and probably as futile.

The failure of the Church to come up with some kind of official liturgy leaves the field wide open for improvisation. Anglican clergy are allowed to devise services to cover needs not met by authorised liturgies, subject only to the Bible and the doctrine of the Church of England. The Bible contains almost nothing on the subject of homosexuality, certainly not as it is understood in contemporary Britain. Men who believe they should observe a ban on anal sex, based on Leviticus 18, do not have to do it. Most married people, straight or gay, don't. But that doesn't prevent them getting married.

Meanwhile, the doctrine of the Church of England is clear in theory but ambivalent in practice, for example about divorcees. At the very least, demand for same-sex marriages has thrown the Church of England in at the deep end, after years of obfuscation, well-meaning deliberate ambiguity, and evasion.

Experience of gay blessing liturgies elsewhere in the world is instructive. Beautiful prayers were produced for blessing relationships, some of them adopted enthusiastically by straight couples. As gay people were allowed to marry, however, it became apparent that a marriage is a marriage, and traditional liturgies, with no more than a couple of words' modification, could simply be used as they stood.

The Churches' other acute question is about clergy who contract same-sex marriages. It cannot credibly be argued that such a situation was ever envisaged by those who drew up the canons of the Church. When the current canon was drafted in 1938 its purpose was simply to exclude divorcees. The canon concerned (B30) is invariably interpreted for heterosexual people descriptively, defining an ideal, rather than prescriptively and exhaustively, to exclude all else. How can it be read differently for homosexuals, without anti-gay discrimination that the Church formally rejected for itself in *Issues in Human Sexuality*?

It is also questionable, to say the least, to hand down summary sentences against clergy without testing their legality, or engaging in due process with a right of appeal. The Church could have included a clause banning clergy from same-sex marriages into the equal marriage legislation, but knew perfectly well it would not be acceptable to Parliament. As things stand it is not entitled to act as though new law on this subject had been made when it had not.

In 1909, in the case of *Bannister v. Thompson*, a court laid down a firm obvious principle in relation to a deceased wife's sister marriage: 'the law cannot very well condemn someone for making a lawful marriage, even if the marriage contradicts the Church's teaching'.[10]

Philip Jones describes the Valentine's Day statement's attempt to make new law on the fly in these terms:

It is hard to argue that the law should regard as immoral, or even as unbecoming and inappropriate, the acquisition of a status that the law itself confers … How can a lawful marriage be regarded as a 'grave offence', or indeed as any offence?[11]

Attempts were also made to discourage gay clergy from marrying by appeals to canonical obedience. These rest on the promise made by all clergy to obey their bishops 'in all things lawful and honest'. It is not, and never has been, 'Episcopal Simon Says'.[12] Rather it is a promise to collaborate with the bishop in enabling the canons of the Church to operate. As such, the concept is broadly and generously interpreted, for example in favour of Evangelical clergy who do not wear the prescribed robes for communion services.

Finally, the 2014 Church of England House of Bishops Valentine's Day statement[13] rather desperately tried to suggest that getting married under the new legislation was a particular form of disciplinary offence – 'conduct unbecoming a clerk in holy orders'. This phrase comes from the Clergy Discipline Measure 2003, and could only normally be applied following particular proceedings. The whole point of these would have been to establish whether some conduct is in fact what it has been alleged to be. Prejudging the issue with no hearing or right of appeal is legal smoke and mirrors.

It would probably be wise to take threats of such action with a large pinch of salt. If bishops sincerely believed a disciplinary offence had been committed it would be their duty to instruct an archdeacon to complain. If they did not, it would be better not to suggest it was possible, in the hope some passing member of the public would do their duty for them.

Such action would not be advisable, for the law concerned states it cannot deal with doctrinal argument, only common immorality. The seventeenth-century canons defined these as

> base or servile labour, drinking or riot, spending their time idly … playing at dice, cards or tables, or any other unlawful games … adultery, whoredom, incest or drunkenness …

swearing, ribaldry, usury and any other uncleanness and wickedness of life.[14]

The colourful seventeenth-century definition of clerical indiscipline was refined by the Church Discipline Act 1840 as improved in 1892 'for punishing those offences which do not depend on disputable points of law, or on matters that are so highly controversial as doctrine and ritual; but which in the consensus of general opinion are acts of personal immorality, such as various forms of vice or dishonesty or other like conduct, of evil example generally, and especially so if committed by a person invested with sacred functions.'[15]

In times past gay clergy had no option to marry. Now they do. Any suggestion the House of Bishops may make that getting legally married is, in itself, an uncontroversial act of common dishonesty and personal immorality (especially compared to, say, living with a boyfriend) is laughable.

The Measure itself says that it cannot deal with matters of doctrine or discipline. The archbishops have consistently said that they regard same-sex marriage as a matter of doctrine. Thus the Clergy Discipline Measure is formally irrelevant. This may explain a puzzling flip within the guidelines, describing same-sex marriage as a disciplinary matter but refusing to prosecute it, instead pushing responsibility for so doing onto gullible members of the public. It is hardly surprising that backtracking statements from various bishops about what they had just signed up to followed hot on the heels of the Valentine's Day statement.

Naturally, gay clergy got married within weeks of the House of Bishops' guidelines. Canon Jeremy Pemberton and Mr Lawrence Cunnington were married on 12 April 2014, and the Revd Andrew Cain became England's first incumbent in a same-sex marriage when he married Mr Stephen Foreshew ten weeks later. From 10 December 2014 provision has been made for civil partners to trade in their status for marriages.

In 2014 the bishops were left all at sea. In spite of the blustering menacing tone of their Valentine's Day statement, there is little they could actually do about established clergy who married. They had to confine active resistance to intimidation aimed at curates and ordinands, who are more vulnerable. The weak were kicked hardest, which in itself was an unedifying sight.

As an alternative to coercion, the Church inaugurated a series of shared conversations on the subject of homosexuality. This could be seen as the reanimation of the moderated discussions that were held in various dioceses a decade before, but in a radically changed context. While no one could criticise the noble intention of getting people together to seek reconciliation, it was not entirely clear who would be talking to whom about what, why, and to what end.

The way conversations were set up tried to protect the principle of talking to people, not about them, by specifying that there should be two openly gay people and two people under 40 in each small group. The process would cascade down from the College of Bishops to regional groups selected by their bishops and, finally, the General Synod. Since everyone in the College of Bishops is well over 40, and it contains no gay people who are out, it remains to be seen how this design will play out in practice.

Facilitated conversations at the turn of the century involved conservatives dialoguing with liberals. The position now has become very much more complicated.

The majority of English Anglicans do not see what the fuss is about, find it uncongenial, and do not wish to talk about the subject. A minority believes it is right to open marriage to gay people on moral grounds. The possibility of doing this has now become the law of England. Since no one is going to force anyone to marry anyone else, there is hardly anything practical to discuss on that score.

Many conservatives and Evangelicals do not feel confident with their former certainties about gays and are modifying their views. A tiny minority of conservative zealots find themselves marginalised about something that was simply assumed in the world in which they grew up. They do not particularly want to talk about this painful experience. The most extreme would say there is nothing to talk about anyway, since their views are simply God's from the Bible. It remains to be seen what positive difference shared conversations will make, if any, to the Church's ability to accept reality.

It may be that this problem will simply resolve itself as time goes by. The English have a strong record of adapting to social reality, mirrored by changes in every field of public life except the Church. Few will want to say anything that they might later regret.

Many Evangelical Christians have a very strong instinct to be good news within the communities they serve. At some point in the future the Church will summon up the courage to talk honestly about this subject, but in 2014, perhaps, it was overwhelmed, like anti-reform Tories who disastrously resisted parliamentary reform in the 1820s using the argument 'It is dangerous to repair one's house in the hurricane season'.[16]

Positive change will come when church authorities decide to stop framing the gay issue as an embarrassing problem. This will involve embracing a positive theology of marriage beyond Janet and John's, drawn from first principles, applied to an ordinance that, since patriarchal times, has always belonged to the present passing age and evolved accordingly.

This is partly a question about distinctiveness, and partly about the terms on which the Church can bring the grace and truth of Christ to a post-Christendom world in which they no longer call all the shots.

Behind pragmatic decisions lie bigger questions. 'Under what circumstances can human relationships be holy?' If God saw all that he had made, and it was good, what are the implications of this for the best life has to offer now? How are people's natural instincts and affections, implanted by God, hallowed and directed aright? If marriage is the highest expression of human love, rather than a dynastic matter or breeding arrangement, how do people discern a calling to it?

What special things can Christians bring to marriage? What makes couples holy? Back in the fifth century, St Augustine pondered the particular meaning of marriage from a Christian perspective. He did not believe married Christians were either more procreative or sexually licensed than anyone else. For him, a Christian vocation to marriage was distinguished by characteristics of permanence, stability and fidelity, reflecting the covenanted grace of God to his people. It was these qualities, not marriages' biological, societal or legal dimensions, that made them Christian.

Augustine's insight has deep roots in Scripture. St Paul spoke of marriage as a mystery that mirrored the love of God for his people. Disciples' marriages should be distinctive, says his letter to the Ephesians, because of the quality of self-giving love between the parties. It adds nothing to our understanding of these biblical images of marriage to view it as difference of gender or breeding of children. These dimensions are subsidiary and incidental, and the tests of discipled marriage in the New Testament can as easily be applied to a same-sex marriage as any other.

Sociological foundations have been shaking in the West for a very long time. The rational-legal institution of marriage instituted in England in the eighteenth century, for which the Church of England was recruiting sergeant and gatekeeper, has evolved. In its place marriage is seen not so much as a societal regulator as the relational gold standard. Those who see it this way are far closer to St Augustine and John Milton than they know.

Marriages that are good news reflect equality in diversity and a genuine reciprocity, their own personal and distinctive complementarity, that is bigger than the imposition of crude gender stereotypes. Such marriages offer a special opportunity for those within them to reflect the values of the kingdom of God within which all are equal. The gold standard for human relationships is not control or hierarchy, but self-giving love. Such love casts out fear, founded on realism about the way we are made, expressing the purpose for which we were made, the wedding feast of the kingdom of heaven.

Notes

Introduction: Outwitted?

1. The whole affair is well documented in Stephen Bates, *A Church at War: Anglicans and Homosexuality*, London, 2004, pp. 160–179.
2. This phrase is from the Declaration of Assent given in canon C15 of the Church of England, https://www.Churchofengland. org/about-us/structure/Churchlawlegis/canons/section-c.aspx (accessed 25/07/2014).

Chapter 1: Gay and straight in Church and State

1. Stephen Cretney, *From 'Odious Crime' to 'Gay Marriage'* (Clarendon Law Lectures), Oxford, 2006.
2. Malcolm Johnson, *Diary of a Gay Priest: The Tightrope Walker*, Alresford, 2013. Entry for 25 September 1986.
3. *Ibid.*, p. 137, a full account of the incident.
4. In June 2008, the Von Hügel Institute published what was rather portentously called 'A Report for the Church of England and to the Nation', complaining that the government suffered from 'deep religious illiteracy', had 'no convincing moral direction' and was showing a 'significant lack of understanding of, or interest in, the Church of England's current or potential contribution in the public sphere'. Francis Davis, Elizabeth Paulhus and Andrew Bradstock, *Moral, But no Compass: Government, Church and the Future of Welfare*, Chelmsford, 2008, pp. 24, 101 and 15.
5. Rowan Williams, *Communion, Covenant and our Anglican Future: Reflections on the Episcopal Church's 2009 General Convention from the Archbishop of Canterbury for the Bishops, Clergy and Faithful of the Anglican Communion,* Pentecost Letter to the Anglican Communion, 27 July 2009, para. 8 (http://www.scifac.ru.ac.za/ cathedral/communion.htm (accessed 27/07/2014).
6. Attempts at progress by deconstructing the issue, like Oliver O'Donovan, *A Conversation Waiting to Begin: The Churches and the Gay Controversy*, London, 2009, achieve little because, well-

meaning as they are, they reduce what has been experienced as personal oppression to an intellectual puzzle. People who are getting soaked in a thunderstorm need waterproofs, not a lecture on global warming, however correct.

7. Paul Fussell, *The Great War and Modern Memory*, Oxford, 1975, pp. 288ff. The author also draws attention to this poem as an example of the 'homoerotic sensuousness' in Owen's poetry.

Chapter 2: Unnatural?

1. Joseph Butler, *Fifteen Sermons Preached at the Rolls Chapel Upon the following Subjects ...,* London, 1726, p. 136, Sermon VII 'Upon the Character of Balaam'.

2. For a theologian's kindly efforts to make sense of the fog of Christian confusion and cultural prejudice in the 1960s and 1970s see Helmut Thielicke, *The Ethics of Sex*, London, 1964, pp. 269–92.

3. Anne Fausto-Sterling, *Sexing the Body: Gender Politics and the Construction of Sexuality*, New York, 2000, p. 35.

4. L. S. Allen, M. F. Richey, Y. M. Chai, R. A. Gorski, 'Sex differences in the corpus callosum of the living human being', *Journal of Neuroscience*, Vol. 11 (1991), pp. 933-42.

5. Information from Facebook conversation with Ann Memmott, Adviser to the All Party UK Parliamentary Group for Autism.

6. Wendy Lawson, *Sex, Sexuality and the Autism Spectrum*, London, 2004, p. 83.

7. A. Chandra, US Department of Health and Human Services, *National Health Statistics Reports 36 (March 3, 2011): Sexual Behavior, Sexual Attraction, and Sexual Identity in the United States: Data From the 2006–2008 National Survey of Family Growth,* www.cdc.gov/nchs/data/nhsr/nhsr036.pdf (accessed 25/07/2014).

8. *Adversus Haereses* IV.20.7 – J.-P. Migne, *Patrlogiae Graecae* VII/1, Paris, 1857, Col. 1037 (my translation).

Chapter 3: Equality or bust

1. Vincent J. Donovan, *Christianity Rediscovered*, Chicago, 1978.

2. H. Richard Niebuhr, *Christ and Culture*, New York, 1951.

3. Theodosian Code 9.7.3, http://ancientrome.ru/ius/library/codex/theod/liber09.htm#7 (accessed 26/07/2014).

4. *OED,* Compact Second Edition Complete Text, Oxford, 1991, p.763, (vol VII. p, 191, col. 1.).

5. 'The condition of being a husband or wife: the relation between married persons; spousehood, wedlock', *OED*, 1991 p. 1039 (vol, IX. p, 396, col. 1).

6. Andrew Foreshew-Cain's Facebook page, https://www.facebook.com/andrew.d.cain?fref=ts, entry for 19 June 2014 (accessed 25/07/2014).

7. Article on *Salon* website, 26 June 2013, http://www.salon.com/2013/06/26/lets_end_gay_marriage/ (accessed 25/07/2014).

8. Claire Jones, *The Art of Uncertainty*, 28 January 2014, http://theartofuncertainty.com/2014/01/28/it-could-have-been-me/ (accessed 25/07/2014).

9. Thomas Merton, *No Man is an Island*, Boston MA, 2005, pp. 177–8.

10. Jane Elliot, *The Angry Eye – All in One*, 2000, video.

11. *Stephen Fry: Out There*, BBC2, first broadcast 14 and 21 October 2013, BBC/Open University co-production, http://www.bbc.co.uk/programmes/p01fttn0 (accessed 25/07/2014).

Chapter 4: Scripture 101

1. Huffington Post, 02/01/2014, 'Pamela Raintree, Transgender Woman Who Dared Councilman To Stone Her, Speaks Out', http://www.huffingtonpost.com/2014/02/01/pamela-raintree-rob-webb-_n_4699226.html (accessed 25/07/2014).

2. Mark Noll, *The Civil War as a Theological Crisis* (The Steven and Janice Brose Lectures in the Civil War Era), Chapel Hill NC, 2006.

3. R. (on the application of Phillip Williamson) v Secretary of State for Education and Employment;[1]UKHL 15 [2005] 2 A.C. 24. Judgment at http://www.parliament.the-stationery-office.co.uk/pa/ld200405/ldjudgmt/jd050224/will-1.htm (accessed 25/07/2014).

4. Harry Potter, *Hanging in Judgment: Religion and the Death Penalty in England from the Bloody Code to Abolition*, London, 1993.

Chapter 5: Things gays are liable to read in the Bible

1. Martha A. Brozyna (ed.), *Gender and Sexuality in the Middle Ages: A Medieval Source Documents Reader,* Jefferson NC, 2005, p. 40.

2. *OED,* Compact Second Edition Complete Text, Oxford, 1991 p. 1817 (vol. XIV, p. 925, col. 3).

3. Francis Brown, S. R. Driver, G. A. Briggs, *A Hebrew and English Lexicon of the Old Testament,* Oxford, 1972 edn, p. 1072, col. 2.

4. Donald Donaldson, 'Rape of Males', in Wayne Dynes (ed.), *Encyclopedia of Homosexuality,* New York, 1990.

5. *De Vit. Abraham* XXVI Nahum N. Glatzer (ed.), *The Essential Philo,* New York, 1971, p. 110.

6. See above, Chapter 2, note 7.

7. Walter Bauer, William F. Arndt and F. Wilbur Gingrich, *A Greek English Lexicon of the New Testament and Other Early Christian Literature* (Fourth Augmented Edition), Chicago, 1957, pp. 489–90. For a full discussion of the term's meaning and use, see K. Renato Lings, *Love Lost in Translation: Homosexuality and the Bible,* Bloomington IN, 2013, pp. 490–501.

8. Bauer, Arndt, Gingrich, *uxicon* pp. 109, 440, and full discussion in Lings, *Love Lost,* pp. 502–14.

9. Milton S. Terry (trans.), *The Sibylline Oracles,* New York and Cincinnati, 1899, Book 2, pp. 84–9 www.sacred-texts.com/cla/sib/sib.pdf (accessed 25/07/2014).

10. J. K. Elliott, *The Apocryphal New Testament: A Collection of Apocryphal Christian Literature in an English Translation Based on M. R. James,* Oxford, 2005: *The Acts of John,* 36. p. 316.

Chapter 6: Biblical marriage

1. Hyde v. Hyde and Woodmansee Law Reports, Probate & Divorce 130, 20 March 1866 (http://www.uniset.ca/other/ths/LRIPD130.html accessed 25/07/2014). The legal academic Rebecca Probert has pointed out that Penzance's Obiter Dictum cannot really be considered to be a definition of marriage at all 'since it is capable of encompassing a large number of persons who are not married while at the same time excluding a significant number of married couples'. (Hyde v Hyde: defining or defending marriage? Child and Family Law Quarterly, vol. 19 No. 3, p. 323.

Chapter 7: The irresistible rise of Christian marriage

1. https://www.Churchofengland.org/media/1879636/ radcliffepresentation.pdf p.1 (accessed 25/07/2014).

2. Philip Lyndon Reynolds, *Marriage in the Western Church: The Christianization of Marriage during the Patristic and Early Medieval Periods*, Boston MA and Leiden, 2001, p. 121.

3. Ibid., p. 254.

4. Roger Virgoe (ed.), *Private Life in the Fifteenth Century: Illustrated Letters of the Paston Family*, London, 1989, p. 186.

5. Quoted in Christopher Brooke, *The Medieval Idea of Marriage*, Oxford, 1989, pp. 278–9.

6. Anne P. Alwis, *Celibate Marriages in Late Antique and Byzantine Hagiography: The Lives of Saints Julian and Basilissa, Andronikos and Athanasia, and Galaktion and Episteme*, London, 2011, p. 93. See also Brooke, *Medieval Idea,* pp. 128–130.

7. Act 1, Scene 3, http://www.gutenberg.org/files/2232/2232-h/2232-h.htm (accessed 25/07/2014).

8. David Loewenstein (ed.), *John Milton Prose: Major Writings on Liberty, Politics, Religion, and Education*, Chichester, 2013. p. 130. (*The Doctrine and Discipline of Divorce Restor'd to the good of both Sexes, from the bondage of Canon Law and other mistakes, to the true meaning of Scripture in the Law and Gospel compar'd*, 1644, cap. 13.)

9. Ibid., p. 111.

10. *Dictionary of National Biography*, vol. XXVIII, Oxford, 1891, pp. 33–4.

11. Matthew Henry, Commentary on Genesis 2:21–5 http://www.studylight.org/commentaries/mhm/view.cgi?bk=0&ch=2 (accessed 25/07/2014).

12. *An Act for the Better Preventing of Clandestine Marriages*, 26 Geo. II, cap. 33.

13. William Cobbett (ed.), The *Parliamentary History of England from the Earliest Period to the Year 1803*, Vol. XV, London, 1813, AD 1753–65, col. 72.

14. A. C. Benson, *The Life of Edward White Benson, Sometime Archbishop of Canterbury*, London, 1899, Vol. 2, p. 12.

15. *The Deceased Wife's Sister's Marriage Act, 1907* (7 Edward VII, cap. 47).

16. G. K. A. Bell, *Randall Davidson, Archbishop of Canterbury*, 3rd edition, London, 1952, p. 552.

17. Letter in *The Times*, 22 August 1907, quoted by William Whyte, 'Why did this seem like a great moral safeguard?', *Church Times*, 31 August 2007, http://www.Churchtimes.co.uk/articles/2007/31-august/comment/why-did-this-seem-like-a-great-moral-safeguard (accessed 27/07/2014).

18. Ibid.

19. *Matrimonial Causes Act, 1937* (1 Edw. VIII and 1 Geo. VI, cap. 57).

20. Appellate Committee of the House of Lords (*Regina v R.* (1991), UKHL 12) after Regina v. Sharples, http://www.bailii.org/uk/cases/UKHL/1991/12.html.

Chapter 8: Geopolitics and Mission

1. http://www.pewglobal.org/2014/04/15/global-morality/table/homosexuality/ (accessed 25/07/2014).

2. Kwame Anthony Appiah, *The Honor Code: How Moral Revolutions Happen,* New York, 2010.

3. Ken Jones, *Alas Poor Heslop: The Last Fatal Duel in Wales*, Newcastle Emlyn, 2007.

4. Sexual Minorities Uganda, Expanded Criminalisation of Homosexuality in Uganda: A Flawed Narrative. Empirical evidence and strategic alternatives from an African perspective, http://76crimes.com/2014/01/30/21-varieties-of-traditional-african-homosexuality/ (accessed 25/07/2014).

5. The most famous instance is Chapter XVI, Section 377 of the Indian Penal Code, which a court refused to set aside in 2014.

6. David A. J. Richards, *The Rise of Gay Rights and the Fall of the British Empire: Liberal Resistance and the Bloomsbury Group*, Cambridge, 2013, p. 221. For more mainline rhetoric, a conference of over 2,000 convened by a group called United For Life at the African Union HQ in Addis Ababa on 9 June 2012 rejected aid from gay-friendly Western nations and announced 'Ethiopia has no room for homosexuality and our country will be the graveyard of homosexuality', http://www.pinknews.co.uk/2012/06/13/leaders-of-ethiopia-call-for-anti-gay-measures/ (accessed 27/07/2014).

7. David J. Bosch, *Transforming Mission: Paradigm Shifts in Theology of Mission*, New York, 2011, p. 10.

8. Ibid., p 11.

9. Interview with Cole Moreton, *Daily Telegraph*, http://www.telegraph.co.uk/news/religion/10775127/The-Archbishop-of-Canterburys-deadly-dilemma.html (accessed 27/07/2014).

10. See, for example, the thoughtful response of the US Episcopalian blogger Mark Harris http://anglicanfuture.blogspot.co.uk/2014/04/the-moral-compass-has-location.html (accessed 27/07/2014).

11. Libby Purves, 'Retreat from your battle against gay marriage', *The Times*, 30 August 2012, http://www.thetimes.co.uk/tto/opinion/columnists/libbypurves/article3302325.ece (accessed 25/07/2014).

12. Ruth Gledhill, 'Justin Welby: "Homosexuality was a 'lightning conductor' in the power struggle between evangelicals and liberals"', *Christian Today*, 26 June 2014, quoting interviews between Justin Welby and Andrew Atherstone, http://www.christiantoday.com/article/justin.welby.homosexuality.was.a.lightning.conductor.in.the.power.struggle.between.evangelicals.and.liberals/38498.htm (accessed 25/07/2014).

13. Jon Kuhrt, 'Going Deeper Together: Resisting Tribal Theology' in *Crossover City: Resources for Urban Mission and Transformation,* London, 2010, pp. 18–19.

Chapter 9: 'The law of the land, and that's great'

1. BBC News UK, 29 March 2014, 'Same-sex marriage now legal as first couples wed' http://www.bbc.co.uk/news/uk-26793127 (accessed 25/07/2014).

2. David Cameron, 'When people's love is divided by law, it is the law that needs to change' in *PinkNews*, 28 March 2014, http://www.pinknews.co.uk/2014/03/28/david-cameron/ (accessed 25/07/2014).

3. David Sylvester, 'I won't resign as a town councillor' in the *Henley Standard*, 20 January 2014, http://www.henleystandard.co.uk/news/news.php?id=39428 (accessed 25/07/2014).

4. Emmanuel Babatunde's Blog, Same-Sex Marriage is Evil – Pastor Adeboye, 23 January 2013, http://www.emmanuelbabatunde.com/2013/01/same-sex-marriage-is-anathema-to-will.html.

5. Justin Welby interview with *PinkNews*, 13 May 2014, 'Exclusive: Archbishop of Canterbury: It's "great" that equal marriage is the law of the land', http://www.pinknews.co.uk/2014/05/13/

exclusive-archbishop-of-canterbury-its-great-that-equal-marriage-is-the-law-of-the-land/ (accessed 25/07/2014).

6. See above, Chapter 2, note 7.

7. Church of England response to the Government Consultation on Equal Marriage, June 2012, para 13, www.Churchofengland.org/media/1475149/s-s per cent20marriage.pdf (accessed 25/07/2014).

8. Letter to Lord Alli, reported by Edward Malnick, *Daily Telegraph*, 30 May 2013, http://www.telegraph.co.uk/news/religion/10087845/Opponents-of-gay-marriage-like-supporters-of-apartheid-says-senior-bishop.html (accessed 25/07/2014).

9. Article in *Halesowen News*, 10 January 2013, http://www.halesowennews.co.uk/news/worcestershire/10154000._/? (accessed 25/07/2014).

10. Philip Jones, Ecclesiastical Law (blog) 'Clergy Discipline and Same-sex Marriage: Inappropriate Conduct?', http://ecclesiasticallaw.wordpress.com/2014/02/19/clergy-discipline-and-same-sex-marriage-inappropriate-conduct/ (accessed 25/07/2014).

11. Ibid.

12. Rupert Bursell QC, 'The Path of Canonical Obedience' *Ecclesiastical Law Journal* 16 (2014), Cambridge, pp. 168–186.

13. https://www.Churchofengland.org/media-centre/news/2014/02/house-of-bishops-pastoral-guidance-on-same-sex-marriage.aspx (accessed 25/07/2014).

14. *Constitutions and Canons Ecclesiastical*, 1603, No. 12, in Richard Burn, *The Ecclesiastical Law* (9th edition), Vol. IV, London, 1842 p. 695.

15. *Church Discipline Act 1840* 3 and 4 Victoria, cap. 86. John Mews (ed.), *The Law Journal reports for the Year 1897. Cases decided by the Judicial Committee and the Lords of Her Majesty's Privy Council and in the House of Lords (Scotch and Irish Appeals)*, vol. LXVI, London, 1897, p. 10.

16. Interview with Lord John Russell, *The Times*, 18 January 1875.